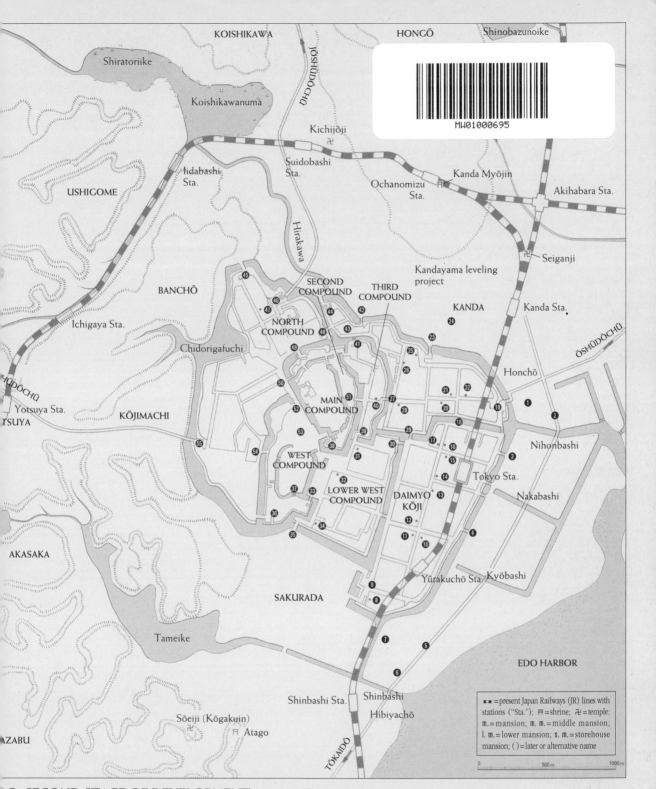

KOISHIKAWA **HONGŌ** Shinobazunoike

Shiratoriike

Koishikawanumà

MW01000695

USHIGOME

Iidabashi Sta.

Suidobashi Sta.

Kichijōji 卍

Ochanomizu Sta.

Kanda Myōjin 卍

Akihabara Sta.

Seiganji 卍

Kandayama leveling project

BANCHŌ

Ichigaya Sta.

Chidorigafuchi

SECOND COMPOUND

THIRD COMPOUND

NORTH COMPOUND

KANDA

Kanda Sta.

Honchō

ŌSHŪDŌCHŪ

Yotsuya Sta.

KŌJIMACHI

ŌSHŪDŌCHŪ

ŌTSUYA

MAIN COMPOUND

Nihonbashi

WEST COMPOUND

Tokyo Sta.

Nakabashi

LOWER WEST COMPOUND

DAIMYO KŌJI

AKASAKA

SAKURADA

Yūrakuchō Sta.

Kyōbashi

Tameike

EDO HARBOR

Shinbashi Sta.

Shinbashi

Hibiyachō

Sōeiji (Kōgakuin) 卍

卍 Atago

AZABU

TŌKAIDŌ

BANCHŌ, Hirakawa, JŌSHŪDŌCHŪ

■■ = present Japan Railways (JR) lines with stations ("Sta."); 〒 = shrine; 卍 = temple; m. = mansion; m. m. = middle mansion; l. m. = lower mansion; s. m. = storehouse mansion; ( ) = later or alternative name

0   500 m   1000 m

DO: SECOND STAGE OF DEVELOPMENT (CA. 1608). From "Keichō 13 [1608] Map of Edo" (*Keichō jūsannen Edo zu*).

...rugachō; 2. Muromachi; 3. Hashi (Gofukubashi); 4. Hashi (Kajibashi); 5. Owarichō; 6. Izumochō; ...gachō; 8.Matsudaira Izu m.; 9. Hibiyamon; 10. Yamanouchi m.; 11. Asano m.; 12. Kyōgoku m.; 13. ...daira Echigo m.; 14. Kuroda m.; 15. Hachisuka m.; 16. Hosokawa m.; 17. Arima m.; 18. Dōsanbori; ...akusabashi (Tokiwabashimon); 20. Maeda m.; 21. Tōdō m.; 22. Ikoma m.; 23. Kandabashimon; 24. ...wachō; 25. Doi m.; 26. Itakura storehouse m.; 27. Ōhashi (Ōtemon); 28. Aoyama Hōki m.; 29. ...inokuchi; 30. Wadakura (Wadakuramon); 31. Torii m.; 32. Hiraiwa m.; 33. Nishinomaruōtemon;

34. Matsudaira Suō m.; 35. Sakuradadobashi; 36. Fukiagemon; 37. Nijūbashi; 38. Hasuikemon; 39. Uchisakuradamon; 40. Sakai Gagaku m.; 41. Hirakawamon (Shimobairinmon); 42. Hitotsubashimon; 43. storehouse m.; 44. (Kijibashimon); 45. Iidachōguchi (Tayasumon); 46. (Shimizumon); 47. Naruse m.; 48. (Takebashimon); 49. Dobashi (Kitahanebashi); 50. Hanebashi (Nishihanebashimon); 51. Ōtedobashi (Gejōbashi); 52. (Yamashitamon); 53. Momijiyama; 54. Dobashi; 55. Hanzōmonguchi

EDO, THE CITY THAT BECAME TOKYO

EDO, THE CITY THAT BECAME TOKYO

An Illustrated History

AKIRA NAITO   Illustrations by **KAZUO HOZUMI**

Translated, Adapted, and Introduced by **H. Mack Horton**

KODANSHA INTERNATIONAL
Tokyo · New York · London

K. Hozumi /'82

The original Japanese version of this book, in two volumes, was published by Sōshisha under the title *Edo no machi* in 1982.

Distributed in the United States by Kodansha America, Inc., 575 Lexington Avenue, New York N.Y. 10022, and in the United Kingdom and continental Europe by Kodansha Europe Ltd., 95 Aldwych, London WC2B 4JF.

Published by Kodansha International Ltd., 17-14 Otowa 1-chome, Bunkyo-ku, Tokyo 112-8652, and Kodansha America, Inc.

First edition, 2003
03 04 05 06 07 10 9 8 7 6 5 4 3 2 1
ISBN 4-7700-2757-5

www.thejapanpage.com

CONTENTS

TRANSLATOR'S INTRODUCTION

Twenty-first century Tokyo is one of the world's great cities, the epitome of cosmopolitan postmodernity. When one stands amid the office buildings of its Maruno-uchi district or the neon bars and restaurants of Shinjuku, it seems inconceivable that the grandparents of some of the older passersby knew next to nothing of New York, Paris, or any of the other great metropolises of the West with which their city is now conventionally compared. And vice versa, when Commodore Perry first arrived in Japan in 1853 to open the nation to foreign trade after more than two centuries of seclusion, few of his American countrymen were aware of Edo, as Tokyo was then known, despite the fact that it was then the most populous city on earth.

This book is devoted to depicting through words and illustrations the early rise of that great Japanese city, focusing predominantly on the years from 1603 to 1867, when Edo served as the capital of the fifteen Tokugawa shogun—warlords who ostensibly served the successive emperors but who actually wielded supreme governing power over the nation. Such was the political, economic, and cultural dominance of the Tokugawa and their city that these years are known to Japanese history as the Tokugawa or Edo period. This was the era when flourished much of what today is considered to be traditional Japanese popular culture, such as woodblock prints, kabuki plays, the geisha of the pleasure quarter, sumo wrestlers, and haiku poets, and when many of the social customs that continue to underlie Japanese life were formed.

But despite the preeminence of the shogun and the samurai who protected Edo castle, these centuries were marked by a gradual increase in the power of the common townspeople (*chōnin*) with whom the warriors shared the Edo capital, and by a growing perception of Japan as a single nation. These centuries are also called the "Early Modern" (Kinsei) period in part for that reason. The gradual movement (always partial to be sure) toward the integration of classes, cultures, and urban spaces constitutes one dominant paradigm by which this period—and this book—may be approached.

When in 1590 the warlord Tokugawa Ieyasu (1542–1616) selected the sleepy village of Edo to be the capital of his newly acquired eight-province eastern domain, he and his advisors were primarily motivated by the desire to establish a stronghold for protecting and extending his power. He himself had come to maturity in the bloody century now known as the Age of the Country at War (Sengoku Jidai, 1467–ca. 1573), a survival-of-the-fittest era of little central authority, and he had achieved his own position by force of arms, at the expense of his neighbors. Edo, therefore, was designed as a "castle town" (*jōkamachi*), protected by stone walls and moats. It was Ieyasu's city, built by him and for him; the commonweal was not an issue, except insofar as it perpetuated his authority and his house.

After the death of Ieyasu's own overlord, Toyotomi Hideyoshi (ca. 1536–98), whose mammoth Osaka Castle was the marvel of the age, Ieyasu defeated his rivals for national hegemony at the battle of Sekigahara in 1600. His new position was legitimized in 1603 when the emperor in the ancient capital of Kyoto appointed him his shogun (military commander-in-chief). Emperors had for centuries been confined to largely ceremonial and cultural roles, being obliged by *force majeur* to delegate actual ruling power to the shogun's military government, two of which had preceded Ieyasu's (the Kamakura Shogunate [1192–1333] based in Kamakura and the Ashikaga Shogunate [1338–1573] based in Kyoto). With Ieyasu's imperial appointment to the shogunal office, the building of Edo Castle became a national project, and he obliged the other warlords (daimyo) to make enormous financial contributions to it, at once strengthening his own power and weakening that of potential rivals. Ieyasu's concern for strong defense was well-founded, for fifteen years after Sekigahara, die-hard opponents challenged him in two Osaka campaigns. But the Tokugawa forces emerged victorious, and there were no further concerted challenges to their authority for the next two centuries and more.

The suzerainty of the Tokugawa was philosophically based upon a system of "rule by status" (*mibun seido*) that mandated a strict social hierarchy of four social classes: warriors (*shi*), farmers (*nō*), artisans (*kō*), and merchants (*shō*) (courtiers, clerics, and outcasts were special categories). Of the three classes of commoners, the farmers—producers of the rice that sustained life—were ranked second only to the samurai rulers (perhaps five percent of the population), while the merchants, who were thought to produce nothing and to dirty their hands with money, were relegated to the bottom. Merchants and artisans lived in the cities and thus were referred to together as townspeople. While there was some social mobility within each class, affiliation to each of the four was hereditary, and movement to a higher one nearly impossible.

The city of Edo was designed to mirror those distinctions in geographical and architectural terms. The greater an individual's importance in the warrior universe, the grander was his residence and the closer it was to the castle. Townspeople, who were not permitted to live in warrior districts, were assigned their own more distant sections on the flats to the east of the castle heights. There, they were further divided by occupation, with tatami makers, for example, living in Tatami District (Tatami-chō) and gunsmiths (*teppōshō*) living in Gun District (Teppōchō). All men were by no means created equal in the Tokugawa cosmos; indeed, warriors were legally permitted to cut down (*kirisute gomen*) commoners who showed disrespect.

The ruler himself lived in the castle's main compound (*honmaru*), which housed his majestic palace and great keep. Ieyasu's son and grandson each rebuilt the great keep, restating in architectural terms the shogun's authority over the city. The third keep, which burned in 1657 and was not rebuilt, was nearly a third again as high as the tallest keep still standing today, that of Himeji Castle in present-day Hyōgo Prefecture. When it reached its early mature form under Iemitsu, the nucleus of the castle was the "inner bastion" (*naikaku*), the most important sections of which were the main, second, third, west, and north compounds, which were protected by a system of moats or canals. The moated Daimyo Kōji area was included as well, where the most important lords lived, in close proximity to their warrior ruler. Beyond this lay the castle town (*jōkamachi*), a much larger fortified area surrounded by an outer moat that reached nearly sixteen kilometers in length. The word "castle" was normally used in reference to the inner bastion, but if construed in its widest sense as the entire fortified and moated part of the town, Edo Castle was twice as big as that of Osaka and possibly the largest castle the world has ever known (Totman, *Politics in the Tokugawa Bakufu* 289, see "Further Reading"). Relentless population growth continually forced the city's boundary outward, however, far beyond the fortified and moated center. Already by the time of Iemitsu's son Ietsuna in 1670, Edo had grown to more than sixty square kilometers.

There were further stratifications within each class. The warrior administration was a combination of the shogunal government (*bakufu*), which wielded national authority, and the daimyo lords, who were the regional administrators of their domains (*han* or *ryō*), the system being accordingly known as *baku-han*. The shogun possessed his own vast lands and a stratified system of personal retainers, consisting of "bannermen" (*hatamoto*), who were mostly enfeoffed and who enjoyed audience privileges with the shogun, and "housemen" (*gokenin*), who were stipendiaries without audience privileges. The approximately 250 daimyo lords (their precise number varied) were stratified as well, consisting of *shinpan* ("related" daimyo), made up of Tokugawa collateral houses, *fudai* ("house" daimyo), who had received their daimyo status from the Tokugawa and had mostly been allied with them before the battle of Sekigahara in 1600, and *tozama* ("outside" daimyo), who had not received their daimyo status from the Tokugawa and who had been either enemies or only recent allies at Sekigahara. The tozama lords constituted the greatest potential challenge to Tokugawa hegemony and therefore had no role in shogunal administration. The daimyo within each group were further stratified by income, those differences being visually represented by, for example, mandated distinctions in the size of their Edo mansions and the designs of their main gates. The townspeople, for their part, included various sub-groups, from fabulously wealthy merchants to day-laborers living hand-to-mouth in tenements.

This system was devoted to an unchanging order and to an ideal harmony, where all people knew their place at all times. Threats to that stratification were eliminated insofar as possible, notably those from foreign thought and trade. The Christian religion, introduced into the country by St. Francis Xavier in 1549 and then spread by Jesuit missionaries supported by Portugal and Franciscans backed by Spain, had by the late 16th century become the faith of thousands, including some daimyo. But in the early 17th century the shogunate prohibited it; then in 1629 it required all citizens to tread on bronze plaques (*fumie*) depicting Christ, Mary, or other Christian figures as a sign that they were not adherents of that faith. The proscription was then expanded to all things foreign, with the shogunate between 1635 and 1641 establishing policies that essentially secluded Japan from the rest of the world. The only official "window on the West" remaining was Nagasaki, where a limited Dutch and Chinese presence was tolerated. Japan did, however, continue to trade with Korea and the Ryukyus.

Internal control over the daimyo lords was tightened at the same time through the inauguration in 1635 of the system of "alternate attendance" (*sankin kōtai*), which required them to build and maintain mansions in the shogun's capital and leave their wives and children there when they returned to their own domains. This system, the details of which underwent later modifications, placed the daimyo under regular shogunal scrutiny, their wives and children in Tokugawa hands as permanent hostages, and their treasuries under constant strain from the massive cost of repeatedly moving their enormous retinues.

The Tokugawa "Great Peace" (Taihei) was conservative and at times cruel; during the Tokugawa years there are said to have been between 100,000 and 200,000 public executions at the Kozukappara execution grounds, one of several maintained by the shogunate. Nevertheless, the status quo proved impossible to maintain. Among the first to change were the samurai themselves. After 1615 there were no more wars to fight, and over the course of the first century of the Edo period the samurai were transformed from raw soldiers into a cultured class of civil administrators, for whom *bun* (literacy and cultural attainment) was as important as *bu* (military arts). According to the Confucian system, loyalty on the part of the ruled was to be matched by a sense of *noblesse oblige* on the part of the ruler, and the Tokugawa regime accordingly began to formulate an ideal of "benevolent rule" (*jinsei*), absolute but just. National hegemony gained, the Tokugawa house government was now a national government, and its policy of benevolent rule *ipso facto* implied a new integrative relationship between the ruler and the ruled, even as it strove to perpetuate their differences. The Tokugawa government gradually began to accept more responsibility for popular welfare, providing disaster relief and funding flood-prevention projects and the construction of the Koishikawa infirmary and sanatorium, a workhouse for the indigent at Ishikawajima, and a variety of parks.

Integration was further spurred by enormous population growth. Edo's population had reached 800,000 or so by 1700, and though three-quarters of the area of the city was devoted to warrior residences, nearly half the population (350,000) were townspeople (the crush of humanity in the townsmen districts was three times that of the densest areas of Tokyo today). More and more of the affairs of this burgeoning group were delegated to its own leaders through a chain of command from three aldermen (*machidoshiyori*) down through headmen (*nanushi*) and five-family groups (*goningumi*). The aldermen and headmen were afforded some samurai rights, another form of class integration. Neighborhoods came to be policed by men appointed from among the townspeople who lived there, and fires were suppressed by townsmen fire brigades which eventually became so effective that they essentially superceded the warriors' own brigades and were called to fight fires in warrior districts and even in Edo Castle itself. And while continuing to issue top-down directives via notice boards throughout the city, the shogunate began taking reciprocal notice of the townspeople's needs expressed via the suggestion box.

These changes were reflected in the city's physical development, which expanded (whether by accident or design) outward from the castle core in spiral fashion. Districts formerly divided by occupation came to be integrated as the tide of immigration from the provinces swelled, and areas like Edobashi that had once been mandated as vacant firebreaks were gradually filled in by the shops and warehouses of townspeople desperate for space, after complex negotiations with the government. James L. McClain has used the history of the development of the Edobashi district as a prime example of the shift from warrior fiat to a "negotiated autocracy" that allowed Edo to remain the shogun's capital even as it developed more and more into a townspeople's city (*Edo and Paris* 131, see "Further Reading"). Likewise water use became more egalitarian. Waterways had originally been planned for the sustenance and defense of the castle and the warriors, with the townspeople receiving only what was left. But as time passed, the great water systems become the townspeople's responsibility and pride.

Nowhere was the pace of integration more visible than in the realm of culture. The rising standard of living among townspeople in particular led, for some, to increasing leisure time and discretionary income. They could spend it in the licensed pleasure quarter of Yoshiwara, dallying with courtesans skilled in music, dress, and the arts of love. Or they might frequent the kabuki theaters, where a new Edo "rough style" of acting (*aragoto*), rich in action and bravado, was being developed. Or they could watch sumo matches. Courtesans, actors, and wrestlers—the pop stars of their day—were portrayed in woodblock prints, which new technologies made both colorful and cheap. Woodblock printing also lowered the price of books, such as the spicy stories of the demimonde by the Osaka writer Ihara Saikaku (1642–93).

The lure of this popular culture of the "floating world" (*ukiyo*) proved irresistible not only to its creators, the townspeople, but also to their samurai overlords. Expected to serve as exemplars of moral behavior, warriors were officially discouraged from visiting the pleasure quarter, but many samurai visited the brothels nonetheless, where they would be asked in the spirit of integration to leave their trademark two swords at the door. Others began to supplement their studies of the Confucian classics with an interest in the newest kabuki plays. Moralistic policy-makers in the shogun's government despaired of curtailing such integration, especially when the shogun himself became a frequent theatergoer. But they drew the line when a lady-in-waiting to Shogun Ietsugu's own mother was discovered having an affair with a handsome actor of romantic roles; both were banished from the city.

But cultural integration was also effected by "high" culture trickling down. Many merchants worked extremely hard to rise in the world, not only through their businesses (some of which had codes of behavior as strict and demanding as those of the samurai) but also through study and self-improvement. As their standard of living rose to parity with that of the warriors, their desire for the culture of the warriors rose as well. Some began learning traditional nō chanting, the tea ceremony, and poetry composition. This acquisition of the polite arts was abetted by increasing literacy (it is estimated that by the end of the Edo period half the men and perhaps 15 percent of women were literate), by the development of printing technologies that changed Japan from a culture of scarce, expensive, and laboriously copied manuscripts to one of cheap and widely available printed books, and by lending libraries. More and more townspeople began rubbing shoulders with samurai at poetry gatherings, and the patronage of such townspeople contributed much to the production of the classic poetry and prose of the age, such as the haiku and travel memoirs of Matsuo Bashō (1644–94), a poet of samurai birth who counted both samurai and merchants among his disciples.

By the turn of the 19th century many samurai doubtless felt that integration had gone altogether too far, for the balance of real power in the capital was tipping more and more in favor of the merchants, who in the warrior universe were supposed to be on the bottom rung of the social ladder. That universe was agrarian, founded on rice and its producers, the farmers, but their own capital, Edo, was in the forefront of modern urbanization and commerce. Whereas the merchant economy was based on currency in gold, silver, copper, and paper, the samurai were paid in fixed stipends of rice, which was both a staple and a medium of exchange. Inexorably the samurai fell into debt to rich merchants, and the shogunal treasury itself grew increasingly depleted. Hard times further spurred integrative forces, as some samurai went to work for merchants or became merchants themselves. Others took wives with high dowries from the merchant class, like English lords marrying the daughters of American financiers. Finally the shogun himself brought in wealthy merchants to advise him on budgetary affairs.

Integrative pressures increased concurrently from abroad. Despite its policy of national seclusion, the shogunate recognized early on that Western advances had Japanese applications, and in 1720 it lifted its ban on the importation of foreign books (except those dealing with Christianity) and encouraged the private study of the Dutch language. Some samurai went to Nagasaki to acquire firsthand "Dutch Learning" (*Rangaku*, from *Oranda*, Japanese for Holland). By the 19th century, writes John Whitney Hall, Japanese intelligentsia in almost every field were influenced by the West (*Japan* 221, see "Further Reading").

This type of abstract foreign influence became menacingly concrete on July 8, 1853, when Commodore Matthew C. Perry appeared at the mouth of Edo Bay with four "black ships" sent by American president Millard Fillmore to force an end to Japan's seclusion. Though many called on the shogunate to resist, it was too late to stem the tide, and within five years a trade treaty was signed, the terms of which favored the West. Perry's arrival rang the death knell for a shogunal supremacy that had for years been compromised by internal forces. The fact that the shogun had no clothes was particularly impressed upon some of *tozama* lords, notably those of the western Satsuma and Chōshū domains, traditionally hostile to the Tokugawa regime.

Seizing on this final demonstration of shogunal impotence, they called for the ouster of the Tokugawa and a return to direct imperial rule under the emperor, whom they would now advise. The fifteenth Tokugawa shogun bowed to the inevitable and resigned in 1867, and in the following year he vacated Edo Castle, for two and a half centuries the symbol of Tokugawa power. It became the new imperial palace of the Emperor Meiji (1852–1912), who moved there from Kyoto. Edo, renamed Tokyo ("Eastern Capital"), was now home both to the heir to Japan's ancient imperial house and to a new government (eventually a constitutional monarchy), which then set out to effect Japan's integration into the modern world.

■　■　■

All premodern personal names are in Japanese order, surname first. But famous historical figures (for whom birth and death dates are selectively provided here) are often familiarly referred to by their given names (e.g., "Ieyasu" for Tokugawa Ieyasu or "Bashō" for Matsuo Bashō). Premodern Japanese used both the lunar and solar calendars, and they numbered years in terms of era dates, several of which might successively be adopted during any one imperial reign. Except for years in which the disjunction between lunar and solar measurement required a thirteenth "intercalary" month, each season lasted exactly three months, with spring falling on the first of the first month, usually about four to six weeks later than January 1 in the West. Hence Commodore Perry's arrival at the mouth of Edo Bay on the third of the sixth month, sixth year of the Kaei era, corresponded to July 8, 1853, by the Gregorian calendar. Premodern weights and measures are explained where necessary in the text. Macrons are deleted over common Japanese words, e.g., Tokyo (Tōkyō), Osaka (Ōsaka), Kyoto (Kyōto), Kyushu (Kyūshū), Shinto (Shintō), shogun (shōgun), daimyo (daimyō), sumo (sumō). The translator would like to thank Lisa Sapinkopf and Michael Brase for their editorial advice and many kindnesses, past and present.

H. Mack Horton

14

EDO, THE CITY THAT BECAME TOKYO

Edo, the City that Became Tokyo

This is the story of Edo, the city now called Tokyo. It began its evolution from a sleepy fishing village to the most populous city on earth when the warlord Tokugawa Ieyasu made it the center of his military domain in the late 16th century.

Eastern Japan, where Edo was located, is divided from the west by a great mountain barrier, and the lands "east of the barrier" (Kantō) were developed much later than those to the west (Kansai), where agricultural techniques from the continent had helped establish thriving farm communities from prehistoric times. The new city of Edo in the east was connected to the old capital of Kyoto via two great roads: the Tōkaidō ("Eastern Sea Highroad"), which ran along the Pacific coast, and the Tōsandō ("Eastern Mountain Highroad"), which pushed through the mountains further inland to the north.

Edo was built on the coast at the eastern end of the Kantō Plain, a sprawling flatland irrigated by Tonegawa River, which flooded whenever there were long periods of rain. The suffering locals personified the river as "Bandō Tarō," "the big boy of Bandō" (Bandō means "East of the Hills," another name for the region). In the eyes of courtly residents of the capital, Kyoto, the Kantō region was forlorn, dangerous, and uncivilized, and a prolonged sojourn there was tantamount to exile. The story of the aristocrat Ariwara Narihira (825–80) is a case in point. Centuries before Edo became a great city, the courtier from Kyoto travelled to this wild eastern region, and as he gazed on the huge river and the forbidding distant silhouette of Mount Tsukuba behind, he caught sight of an unfamiliar bird. On learning that it was locally known as a "bird of the capital" (*miyakodori*), he composed this 31-syllable *waka* poem:

> If, as your name implies,
> you are a "bird of the capital,"
> please tell me this:
> is the one I love back home
> still alive, or not?

This simple poem became one of the most famous evocations of lonely travel through that isolated area.

Urbane courtiers from the capital considered themselves a higher order of humanity than the eastern locals, whom they called *azuma ebisu*, "eastern barbarians." But those "barbarians" were also skilled horsemen and proud,

tough fighters, and when they later entered the service of the central government, the magnificent "Bandō warriors" were valued as allies and feared as foes. It was these very Bandō warriors who at the end of the 12th century helped one warrior general, Minamoto Yoritomo (1147–99), wrest ruling power from his courtly superiors in the Kyoto capital. The emperor had no choice but tacitly to recognize Yoritomo's might, and he accordingly appointed him shogun, military commander-in-chief. The new shogun established his government in the Kantō town of Kamakura, to be near his military power base. The emperor remained with his court in the ancient capital of Kyoto, where he reigned as a revered icon but without the real power of his ostensible servant, the shogun. The establishment of Yoritomo's Kamakura Shogunate marked the end of Japan's classical Heian age and the beginning of the bellicose medieval era (ca. 13th to 17th centuries).

It was exactly at this time that the name Edo, then a small village, first appears in historical records. A small castle was built there in the middle of the 15th century that was subsequently expanded by Tokugawa Ieyasu, who founded a later warrior government, the Tokugawa (or Edo) Shogunate, in 1603. Under Ieyasu and subsequent generations of Tokugawa leaders, the town of Edo grew to become what was at that time the largest city not only in Japan but in the entire world.

This book intends to trace the history of the city of Edo, largely in terms of its construction. It is a story of glorious feats, but also of sad failures, a fragile process of trial and error that eventually gave rise to the megalopolis of today.

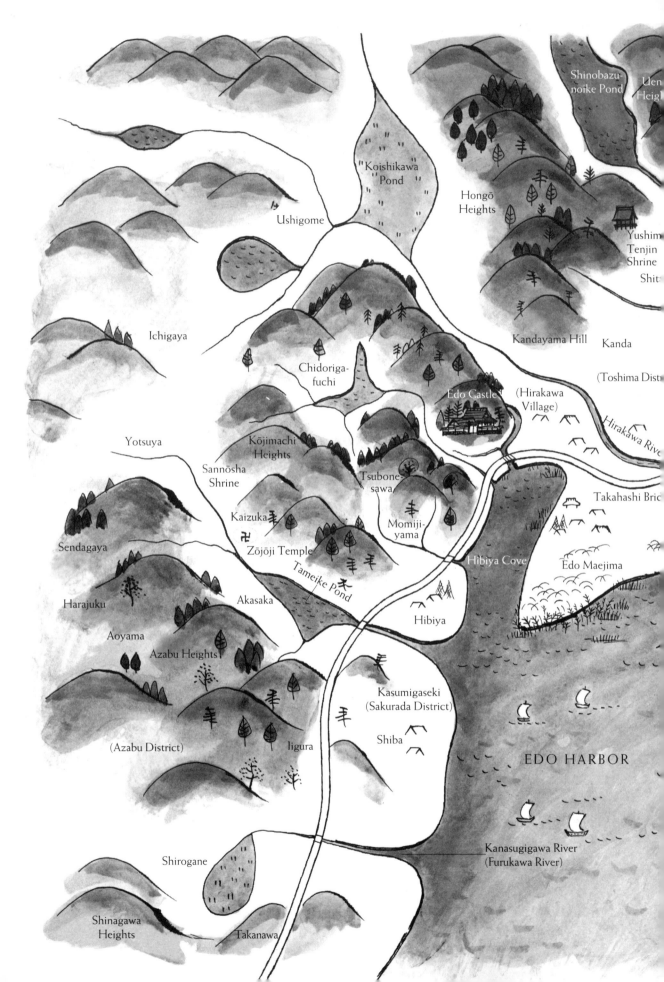

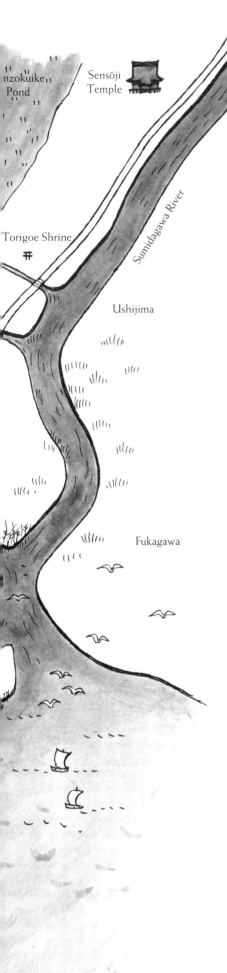

nzokuike
Pond

Sensōji
Temple

Torigoe Shrine

Sumidagawa River

Ushijima

Fukagawa

Primeval Edo

Edo, which means "bay door," was the name of the tract of low wetland where Sumidagawa River flows into what is now Tokyo Bay. To the west stretches the great Kantō Plain, traditionally called Musashi Plain. The plain was once nothing but a seemingly endless expanse of reeds and pampas grass, as described in this old *waka*:

> At Musashi Plain
> the moon has no mountains
> to set behind—
> it comes forth from grasses
> and into grasses sinks from sight.

The plain is punctuated by five rises, called, from west to east, Shinagawa, Azabu, Kōjimachi, Hongō, and Ueno. Running between them are valleys, marshes, and rivers that form various inlets where they converge on what was then Edo Harbor. The largest is Hibiya Cove, which thanks to its extensive shallows and gentle waves was a rich source of edible sea plants. The name Hibiya, in fact, is thought to come from the bamboo structures (*hibi*) used for cultivating sea plants there. The east coast of Hibiya Cove is a peninsula called Edo Maejima. To the north flows Hirakawa River, near which some of the region's earliest inhabitants built the town of Hirakawa. In the 12th century a fort was built here, on the east side of Kōjimachi Heights facing the river, by Edo Shigenaga, a local chieftain said to have made signal contributions to the founding of the Kamakura Shogunate under Minamoto Yoritomo.

Ōta Dōkan's Edo Castle

Fifteenth-century Edo was controlled by Uesugi Sadamasa (1443–94), who served the Kyoto-based Ashikaga shogun as Kantō deputy (*Kantō kanrei*). In 1457, Ōta Dōkan (1432–86), one of Sadamasa's principal retainers, constructed a new castle on the site of Edo Shigenaga's old fortress. Built on a prominence overlooking Hibiya Cove, the castle was protected by moats that exploited surrounding depressions such as Tsubonesawa. It was composed of three compounds: the main Chūjō compound, the subsidiary Shijō compound, and the outer Gejō compound. These constructions correspond to the main compound (*honmaru*), second compound (*ninomaru*), and third compound (*sannomaru*) in Tokugawa Ieyasu's later castle. The central element of Dōkan's main Chūjō compound was his personal living quarters, named Seishō-ken Cottage, together with such subsidiary structures as Gansetsu Studio, with a view of snow-capped Mount Fuji, and Hakusentei Pavilion, overlooking the boats in Hibiya Cove. The Shijō and Gejō compounds also held a variety of structures, including

Edo Castle

large numbers of storehouses and stables together with two towers and five stone gates. It was the most famous castle in the entire Kantō area at the time. Meanwhile, the Kyoto capital was being nearly entirely destroyed in the catastrophic Ōnin civil war of 1467–77. Numerous aristocrats and monks abandoned the ruined capital to take refuge in Dōkan's Edo Castle in the east.

The nearby village of Hirakawa on the southern bank of Hirakawa River, meanwhile, was growing into a bustling "castle town" (jōkamachi). The mouth of Hirakawa River, spanned by the impressive Takahashi Bridge, was likewise becoming a prosperous harbor. Through it flowed products from all over the country, not only staples like rice, tea, and fish, but also occasional rarities like medicines imported from China.

But this prosperity was short-lived, for in 1486 Ōta Dōkan was assassinated at the order of his own overlord, Uesugi Sadamasa. His empty castle town eventually reverted to desolate countryside.

Tokugawa Ieyasu's Arrival in Edo

On the first day of the eighth month (mid-autumn by the old lunar calendar) of 1590, Tokugawa Ieyasu took formal possession of Edo Castle. The event marked the beginning of Ieyasu's campaign to put the entire Kantō region under his control, and it was observed as a memorial day thereafter by successive Tokugawa leaders.

The route for Tokugawa Ieyasu's ultimate success had been paved by his own overlord, Toyotomi Hideyoshi, who had established initial hegemony over the nation by defeating the Hōjō (or Go-Hōjō) house at Odawara in 1590. Hideyoshi marked the role of Ieyasu's part in the victory by conferring on him the Hōjō domain of all eight Kantō provinces: Musashi (Tokyo Metropolitan Prefecture and Saitama Prefecture), Sagami (Kanagawa Prefecture), Awa (Chiba Prefecture), Kazusa (Chiba Prefecture), Shimōsa (Chiba Prefecture and Ibaraki Prefecture), Hitachi (Ibaraki Prefecture), Kōzuke (Gunma Prefecture), Shimotsuke (Tochigi Prefecture),

On the other hand, Hideyoshi relieved Ieyasu of the provinces of Suruga (Shizuoka Prefecture), Tōtōmi (Shizuoka Prefecture), Mikawa (Aichi Prefecture), Kai (Yamanashi Prefecture), and Shinano (Nagano Prefecture). The switch was not a blessing for

Ieyasu, since it purposely distanced him from his traditional power base and forced him into an underdeveloped farther from Kyoto, still the cultural center of the country. Ieyasu's own generals, Honda Tadakatsu, Sakakibara Yasumasa, and Ii Naomasa, all opposed the move, but Ieyasu overruled them and submitted to Hideyoshi's directive. Not only that, rather than establishing himself in an already developed Kantō urban center, such as Kamakura or Odawara, he chose the minor village of Edo, which lay ever farther east. Doubtless he recognized the developmental potential of Ōta Dōkan's old castle town, with its fine bridge and harbor, and all Musashi Plain beyond.

When Ieyasu took possession, Edo Castle was in ruins. Not a single stone wall was left standing, only earthen embankments; what buildings remained were roofed in wooden shingles, like simple village structures. Compared to Hideyoshi's splendid Osaka Castle or to Azuchi Castle of Hideyoshi's predecessor Oda Nobunaga (1534–82), both of which glittered with gold appointments, Ieyasu's new headquarters seemed a miserable affair indeed. But for the moment he was content. After carrying out basic repairs to stop the leaks, he began making plans for a new castle complex and town of enormous proportions.

Principles of Premodern City Planning

Castles in the medieval era were built for protection from the enemy in time of war, and they were generally situated on easily defensible hilltops and known as "mountain castles" (*yamajiro*). But such locations were unsuitable for governing, encouraging production and trade, or enriching city life. In the late 16th century (known as the Azuchi-Momoyama period, 1568–1603), therefore, castles came to be more often built on smaller promontories ("flatland-hill castles," *hirayamajiro*) or on level ground ("flatland castles," *hirajiro*). The castles of both Oda Nobunaga and Toyotomi Hideyoshi, the two greatest late-medieval warlords before Ieyasu, both of whom aimed at national domination, were of the flatland type. Since Ieyasu planned to rebuild Dōkan's older structure, he had no choice but to retain its flatland-hill design, but the surrounding castle town would be situated insofar as possible on the flats below.

In keeping with Ieyasu's hegemonic goals, the direct model for the city of Edo was the old Kyoto capital, established in 794 as a quarter-sized version of the Tang Chinese capital of Changan. The Chinese capital had been laid out through divination according to centuries-old notions of the interaction between the bipolar principles of *yin* (female, dark, cool, moist) and *yang* (male, light, warm, dry), together with elements of what we today would refer to as astronomy and geography, in order to determine a site and orientation most conducive to prosperity.

The geomantic principles of yin-yang theory required a city to be located on a site that answered the requirements of the gods of the four directions. Those requirements were: a river for the Cyan Dragon in the east, a lake or ocean for the Vermilion Bird in the south, a road for the White Tiger in the west, a mountain for the Dark Warrior in the north.

White Tiger (Road)

Tōkaidō Highroad

EDO HARBOR

If those requirements were met, it was thought, a city would provide an ideal living environment, with a mountain behind it to the north, a view of a lake or ocean to the south, a river to the east that would sparkle in the rising sun and provide drinking water, and a road to the west to bring in food. In the case of the Kyoto capital, for example, Kamogawa River flows to the east, Ogura Lake lies to the south, the San'yōdō Highroad runs off to the west, and Mount Funaoka stands to the north.

Edo satisfied these requirements. With hills to the west and Hibiya Cove to the south, the city's projected path of development would be toward the north and east, which slightly skewed the ideal north-south axis between the Dark Warrior and the Vermilion Bird. Edo's east-northeast axis determined the orientation of the Main Gate (Ōtemon) of Edo Castle. Hirakawa River ran to the east in the realm of the Cyan Dragon, and beyond Sumidagawa River lay Edo Harbor, satisfying the requirement of the Vermilion Bird. The Tōkaidō Highroad led to the west, as necessitated by the White Tiger, and Mount Fuji, as seen from Kōjimachi Heights, rose up in the north for the Dark Warrior. Reminders of the plan remain today in such place names as Toranomon (Tiger Gate) and Tatsunokuchi (Dragon Mouth).

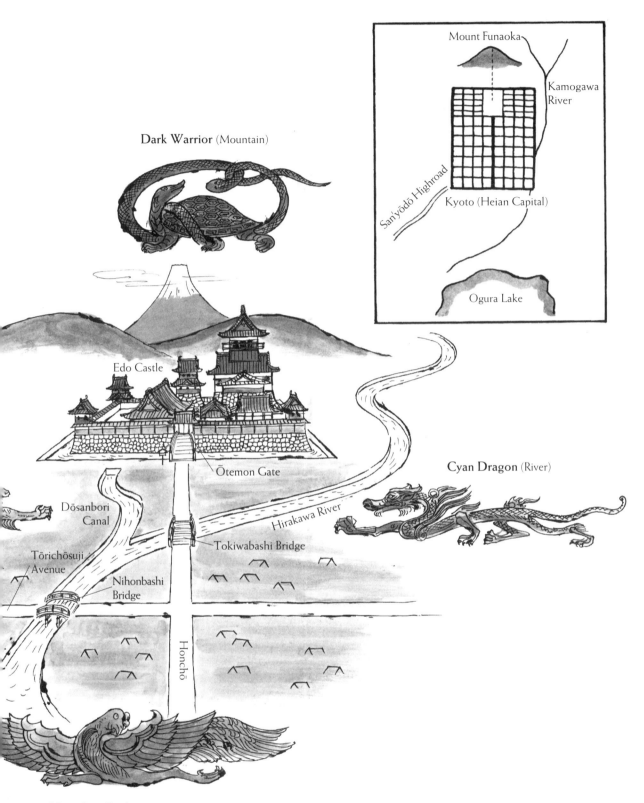

Dark Warrior (Mountain)

Mount Funaoka

Kamogawa River

San'yōdō Highroad

Kyoto (Heian Capital)

Ogura Lake

Edo Castle

Ōtemon Gate

Cyan Dragon (River)

Dōsanbori Canal

Hirakawa River

Tokiwabashi Bridge

Tōrichōsuji Avenue

Nihonbashi Bridge

Honchō

Vermilion Bird (Ocean)

Construction Begins

ken stick

water rope

Meeting the requirements imposed by the gods of the four directions entailed massive restructuring of the natural environment. Ieyasu had, of course, carefully explored the topography before selecting Edo as his castle site. When he took up residence in the province, he built a small cottage in front of what would be Ōtemon Gate, where Kihara Yoshitsugu and his son Shigetsugu would draw up the detailed plans. At the same time, he appointed Amano Saburobei Yasukage as the first city magistrate of Edo (*Edo machi bugyō*) and made him the general overseer of the construction project. Amano was soon succeeded by Itakura Katsushige, who supervised the work of Fukushima Tamemoto as magistrate of construction (*fushin bugyō*) and Tagami Morishige as magistrate of surveys (*jiwari bugyō*). Under these men the building of Edo began in earnest.

Surveying consists of measuring direction and distance. Edo was initially planned before the magnetic compass came into use in Japan, and it appears that north was determined by the traditional method of fixing on the Pole Star. During the daylight hours, north was determined by a method based on the shadow cast by a vertical pole; north was indicated when the shadow was at its shortest. Since this method was only approximate, a different technique was used when a more exact measurement was necessary. At the appropriate time in the morning, an arc was drawn using the base of the pole as the center point and the length of its shadow as the radius. In the afternoon, when the end of the shadow again reached the previously delineated arc, the angle between the morning and afternoon measurements could be bisected, indicating north. Once north was fixed, twelve more directions could be determined at thirty-degree intervals; these were named after the twelve zodiacal signs or "branches" (rat, ox, tiger, hare, dragon, snake, horse, sheep, monkey, bird, dog, and boar; see illustration). North corresponded to the rat, east to the hare, south to the horse, and west to the bird. Further subdivisions could be added according to a related system using some of the "ten stems" (elder brother of wood [*kinoe*], younger brother of wood [*kinoto*], elder brother of fire [*hinoe*], younger brother of fire [*hinoto*], elder brother of earth [*tsuchinoe*], younger brother of earth [*tsuchinoto*], elder brother of metal [*kanoe*], younger brother of metal [*kanoto*], elder brother of water [*mizunoe*], and younger brother of water [*mizunoto*]).

Distance was measured in units of *shaku* (about 30.3 cm) and *ken*, which in Kyoto (the so-called Kyoto ken or *kyōma*) measured 6.5 shaku (about 1.97 m). These measurements were marked on a "ken stick" (*kenzao*) or a "water rope" (*mizunawa*). The *ken* stick was employed when the distance was less than two *ken*; beyond that, builders resorted to the water rope, 5 mm thick and cured with astringent persimmon juice.

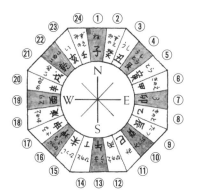

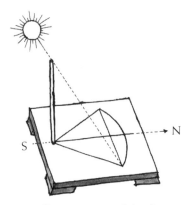

Determining north by the shadow cast by a stick.

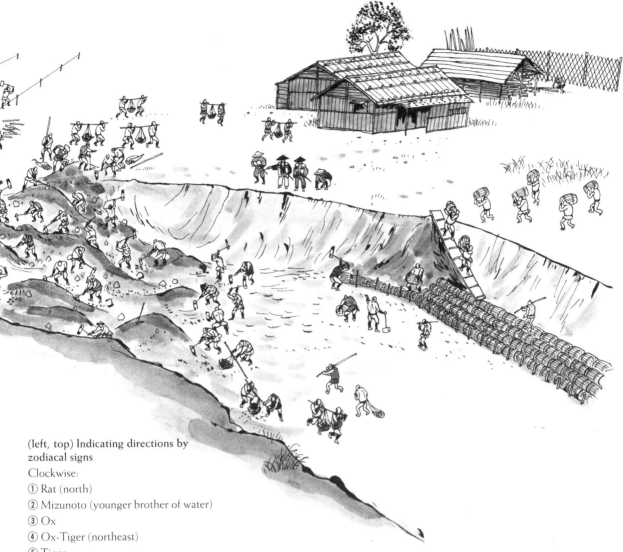

(left, top) Indicating directions by zodiacal signs
Clockwise:
① Rat (north)
② Mizunoto (younger brother of water)
③ Ox
④ Ox-Tiger (northeast)
⑤ Tiger
⑥ Kinoe (elder brother of wood)
⑦ Hare (east)
⑧ Kinoto (younger brother of wood)
⑨ Dragon
⑩ Dragon-Snake (southeast)
⑪ Snake
⑫ Hinoe (elder brother of fire)
⑬ Horse (south)
⑭ Hinoto (younger brother of fire)
⑮ Sheep
⑯ Sheep-Monkey (southwest)
⑰ Monkey
⑱ Kanoe (elder brother of metal)
⑲ Bird (west)
⑳ Kanoto (younger brother of metal)
㉑ Dog
㉒ Dog-Boar (northwest)
㉓ Boar
㉔ Mizunoe (elder brother of water)

These instruments were used to establish the position of roads and canals or moats according to the layout called for in the plans. The canals were particularly important, since they were critical for moving building supplies and daily necessities. The first canal to be built was Dōsanbori, which ran from the mouth of Hirakawa River to a point near the main gate of Edo castle. It was followed by Onagigawa River to the east of Sumidagawa River, used to transport salt from Gyōtoku (in modern Chiba Prefecture).

Drinking water was also a problem. Since Edo was near the ocean, most wells did not provide fresh water. A waterway was therefore run from Koishikawa Marsh in the northern section of the city, which became the beginning of the Kanda water system (Kanda Jōsui). A second system drew its water from Tameike Pond. Thanks to such huge construction projects, Edo was able to accommodate a steadily growing population.

The Layout of Subdivisions

Depending on their occupations, the residents of Edo lived in subdivisions designated for warriors, for clerics, or for townspeople. Warrior families who had moved to Edo from old Tokugawa domains such as Mikawa (Aichi Prefecture) or Tōtōmi (Shizuoka Prefecture) were dispersed to various sites throughout the new castle town, building their mansions (*bukeyashiki*) in such places as the bank of Hirakawa River in front of Ōtemon Gate. In particular, the heights to the north and the west were favored locations for the residences of officials and the tenements (*nagaya*, lit., long houses) of lower-ranking samurai, with several units under one roof.

Districts for Buddhist temples and Shinto shrines were in principle built on important routes. Temples and shrines originally located in the villages of Hirakawa or Tsubone-sawa were all moved to busier sites such as Kandadai Heights and Yanokura.

Townspeople's districts included Dōsanbori at Ōtemon Gate as well as the area east of Tokiwabashi Bridge (the new name for Takahashi Bridge), a bustling spot since Dōkan's day. This area became the commercial center of the castle town and was therefore called Honchō (Central District).

Honchō was laid out after the fashion of the old Kyoto capital to encourage the same prosperity that Kyoto had enjoyed. The basic unit of area was the *chō*, a square of forty *jō* (about 121.2 m) per side, with all four sides composed of townhouses (*machiya*) facing out on the streets. Behind them, in the center of each square, was a common (*kaishochi*) with latrines and garbage facilities for general use. The width of roads was also based on the Kyoto standard, with Honchōdōri Avenue and the other major road that intersected it, Tōrichō-suji (Nihonbashi Avenue) being fixed at six jō (about 18.2 m), and the smaller sidestreets being set variously at four jō (about 12.1 m), three jō (about 9.1 m), or two jō (about 6.1 m). Some critics felt that the allotments were altogether too spacious, since the roads in most castle towns were only two kyōma (about 3.9 m) or at best three kyōma (about 5.9 m) in width. They complained that the generous size of the streets would distance people from storefronts and make them less likely to shop, thus retarding economic growth. The blocks of Ieyasu's city were also larger than the norm for castle towns, again suggesting the grandeur of his plans for his capital.

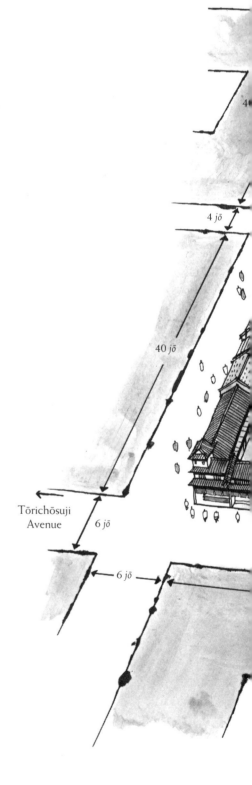

4

4 jō

40 jō

Tōrichōsuji
Avenue

6 jō

6 jō

Honchōdōri Avenue

4 jō

Common

Common

4 jō

40 jō

Bustling Dōsanbori

The first part of the town to develop was the area along Dōsanbori Canal. Subdivisions of this new city center soon grew up on both sides of the canal, like Zaimokuchō for lumber, Funechō for shipping, and Yokkaichichō as a market. Zaimokuchō was lined with shops dealing in lumber from all over Japan, brought in by ship from Edo Harbor and then Nihonbashigawa River and Dōsanbori Canal. Funechō was the site of the concerns that ran the shipping trade. And Yokkaichichō was the market where people from neighboring villages brought in staples for sale.

In this way Ieyasu involved the locals in his urban vision and invited other towns-people to relocate there from Suruga, Tōtōmi, Mikawa, Kai, and more distant areas like Kyoto, Fushimi, Nara, Osaka, and Sakai.

The upper reaches of Sumidagawa River, called Arakawa River, were spanned by Senju Ōhashi Bridge in 1594, followed by Rokugō Bridge over Tamagawa River in 1600. Edo was developing into the center of a transportation network reaching to the far northeast via the Ōshūdōchū Highroad and to the west via the Tōkaidō Highroad. Within ten years of Ieyasu's move to Edo, the groundwork was laid for its development into a great urban center.

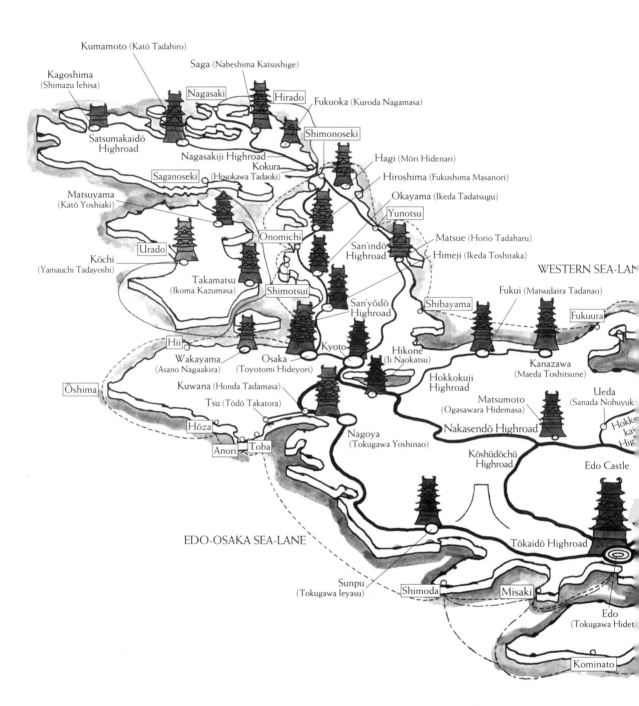

Japan during the rule of Tokugawa Hidetada (1605–23), showing major sea-lanes, high-roads, cities, and castle towns (with the name of each castle's lord in parentheses)

The Founding of the Tokugawa Shogunate

In the eighth month of 1598, the great warlord Toyotomi Hideyoshi, who had defeated many rival daimyo and achieved hegemony over the nation, died at his Fushimi Castle south of Kyoto. His demise sparked a protracted succession struggle that came to a head in the ninth month of 1600, when the Eastern Army of Tokugawa Ieyasu engaged in battle at Sekigahara the Western Army, an alliance of Hideyoshi sympathizers who were threatened by Ieyasu's growing power. At the time Edo Castle was still under construction and without a keep. Comparing it to the magnificence of the Western Army's Osaka Castle with its soaring five-story keep, so grand that it was said to be the greatest fortress, unsurpassed not only in Japan but in China and India as well, few would have doubted that the Western Army would win.

But the Eastern Army was unified, whereas the Western Army was lax and divided by internal dissent, and Ieyasu emerged victorious, becoming the new de facto ruler of the nation. The emperor accordingly appointed him shogun, and the rest of the great lords rendered him fealty. This occurred in the second month of 1603.

Having made peace by force of arms, Ieyasu's next task was to formulate policies to enforce it throughout the country. The first great step was to determine the site for his warrior government. Kyoto was still the spiritual, cultural, and political center of the country, as it had been for centuries, and it was therefore a daring gamble for Ieyasu to decide to locate his own government in Edo, the construction of which had barely gotten underway. On Tōrichōsuji Avenue, which intersected with Edo's central Honchō district, he built Nihonbashi ("Japan Bridge"), which would be reckoned as the point of origin for five great highroads fanning out across Japan (the Tōkaidō, running west along the Pacific to Kyoto; the Nakasendō, running north then west; the Kōshūdōchū, running northwest through Kōshū [Yamanashi Prefecture]; the Ōshūdōchū, running to Ōshū in the far northeast; and the Nikkōdōchū, which forked off from Ōshūdōchū to Nikkō). These great highroads tied into the older network centering in Kyoto, bringing all Japan's castle towns into a single network under the rule of Ieyasu's new military government.

Matsumae

Ajigasawa

Aomori

Hirosaki (Tsugaru Nobumaki)

Hachinohe

Noshiro

Morioka
(Nanbu Toshinao)

Tsuchizaki

Akita (Satake Yoshinobu)

Miyako

Sakata

Sendai
Matsumaedō
Highroad

Ogi

Ushūkaidō
Highroad

Niigata

Aizudōri

ada
sudaira Tadateru)

Sendai
(Date Masamune)

Ishinomaki

kunidōri

Aizu
(Gamō Tadasato)

Arahama

ōdōchū
Highroad

Yonezawa
(Uesugi Kagekatsu)

ūdōchū Highroad

Hirakata

Nakaminato

EASTERN SEA-LANE

Chōshi

A Spiral Plan for the New City

When Tokugawa Ieyasu's rule was formalized by his appointment as shogun, Edo Castle and the city around it instantly became a national center, and planning for massive expansion became necessary. The original plan, based as we have seen on a four-directional scheme borrowed from Kyoto and thence from China, naturally was considerably altered in the process. The new scenario would be for the city to expand in spiral fashion. Edo Castle would be at the center, and canals would spiral out from it clockwise.

But this new plan by no means required the abandonment of the city as it had developed thus far. Instead, the old plan would be incorporated into the new, with outlying hills, valleys, and rivers being gradually exploited to enlarge the canal system in spiral fashion. Following this plan, civil engineers could expand the city almost indefinitely.

The spiral canal system was incorporated into the preexisting plan of five radiating great roads. Thus, no matter how big Edo grew, the warrior districts in the city could continue to be supported by robust free enterprise in the townspeople's districts.

This plan was an innovative solution with few, if any, precedents either in Japan or elsewhere. Thanks to the plan's amenability to growth, the shogunate could effectively impose its system of "alternate attendance" (*sankin kōtai*), wherein the daimyo were required to build residences in the city and leave their wives and children there as hostages even when the lords themselves left for periodic tours of their home domains. There would always be room in the city, no matter how many warriors came to live there. Had this system of spiral expansion not been invented, Edo would probably never have grown as large as it ultimately did.

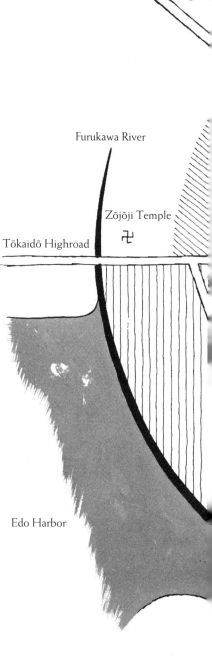

Ōyama Highroad

Furukawa River

Zōjōji Temple 卍

Tōkaidō Highroad

Edo Harbor

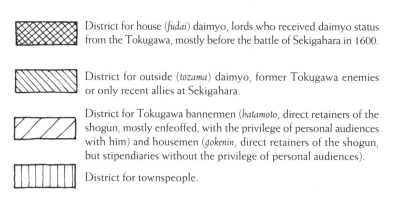

District for house (*fudai*) daimyo, lords who received daimyo status from the Tokugawa, mostly before the battle of Sekigahara in 1600.

District for outside (*tozama*) daimyo, former Tokugawa enemies or only recent allies at Sekigahara.

District for Tokugawa bannermen (*hatamoto*, direct retainers of the shogun, mostly enfeoffed, with the privilege of personal audiences with him) and housemen (*gokenin*, direct retainers of the shogun, but stipendiaries without the privilege of personal audiences).

District for townspeople.

Marks the plan for the city in 1602 (see pp. 24–25).

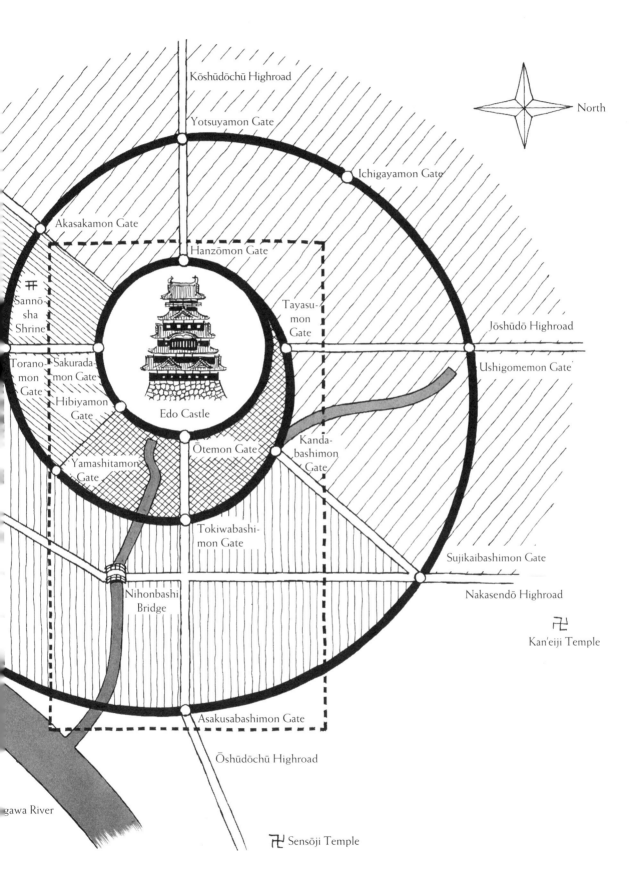

Kōshūdōchū Highroad

Yotsuyamon Gate

Ichigayamon Gate

North

Akasakamon Gate

Hanzōmon Gate

Sannō-
sha
Shrine

Tayasu-
mon
Gate

Jōshūdō Highroad

Torano-
mon
Gate

Sakurada-
mon Gate

Ushigomemon Gate

Hibiyamon
Gate

Edo Castle

Kanda-
bashimon
Gate

Yamashitamon
Gate

Ōtemon Gate

Tokiwabashi-
mon Gate

Sujikaibashimon Gate

Nakasendō Highroad

Kan'eiji Temple

Nihonbashi
Bridge

Asakusabashimon Gate

Ōshūdōchū Highroad

...gawa River

Sensōji Temple

Improving Edo Harbor

While his overlord Toyotomi Hideyoshi was alive, Ieyasu carried out little of the projected construction of Edo Castle except for a part of the west compound (*nishino-maru*). But after Hideyoshi died and Ieyasu was appointed shogun, he could, without fear of reprisal, order any and all daimyo to take part in making his castle the greatest in the land. Its construction thus became a national project.

By way of preparation for this enormous task, work was begun in the third month of 1603, the very next month after Ieyasu was appointed shogun, to regularize the coastline of Edo Harbor and build wharves in order to offload the stone and lumber requisitioned from various parts of the country for the building project.

Then earth from Kandayama Hill was used to fill in the shallows of Hibiya Cove, based on the plan for spiral expansion. At the same time, to the east a canal was dug through Suzaki (Edo Maejima) to connect to Dōsanbori Canal and Hirakawa River, which was renamed Horikawa. The huge Nihonbashi Bridge, the point of origin of Japan's five great highroads, spanned this new waterway.

The size of each daimyo's contribution to this national project was determined by his income. For every thousand *koku* of rice (one koku being equal to about 180 liters or 5 bushels) of his stipend, a daimyo was required to contribute ten men to the building project, and these laborers were therefore called "thousand koku men." The land from Hamachō in Nihonbashi to Shinbashi was filled in, and the districts (*chō* or *machi*) established on the new land were named after the domains that had contributed to their construction: for example, Owarichō, Kagachō, and Izumochō.

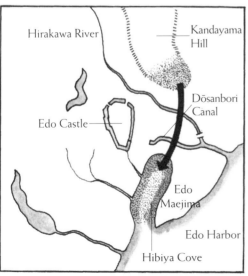

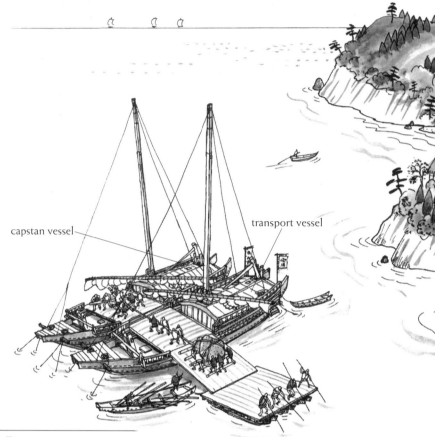

capstan vessel

transport vessel

Quarrying Stone in Izu Province

In 1604 the Tokugawa Shogunate publicly announced its plans for the enormous Edo Castle construction project. The lords ordered to provide the stone for the massive castle foundation walls—among them Ikeda Terumasa (Himeji), Fukushima Masanori (Hiroshima), Kuroda Nagamasa (Fukuoka), and Katō Kiyomasa (Kumamoto)—were all tozama daimyo who had served Hideyoshi before fighting on Ieyasu's side at Sekigahara. Over the next two years, each daimyo readied three or four hundred vessels to transport the stone, and in 1606 the project was begun. The stone, being scarce in Kantō, had to be quarried in Izu (Shizuoka Prefecture), and large numbers of stonemasons together with Tokugawa retainers were needed to do the work.

At the quarries, the stonemasons used hammers and chisels to drive holes into the great rock faces and extract blocks weighing up to several tons. These were pulled by sledge to the coast, where they were inspected at an official checkpoint then loaded onto transport vessels by means of special boats equipped with capstans to haul the enormous blocks on board. A transport vessel could normally handle only two of the blocks, one of which was said to require 100 men to move, and a roundtrip to Edo and back took two weeks. A grand total of three thousand ships were requisitioned from the various daimyo to complete the task.

But the voyage to Edo involved its own share of dangers; Nabeshima Katsushige lost 120 ships during the project, Katō Yoshiaki, 46, and Kuroda Nagamasa, 30.

pulling a sledge
to the coast

official checkpoint

tugboat

rock hammer (*gennō*)

chisel

39

guiding logs
downstream

sluice

Cutting Lumber in the Kiso Mountains

The lumber for the construction project came from the forests near the upper reaches of rivers such as Tonegawa in north Kantō, Fujigawa in Shizuoka Prefecture, and Kisogawa in Nagano Prefecture. The last area in particular had long been famous for the excellent quality of its cypress (*hinoki*).

It was the responsibility of the foremen (*somagashira*) to locate trees that fit the dimensions ordered by the carpenters. The trees were then cut down, trimmed, and transported by sluices down the valleys to the rivers.

Inuyama Castle

Ise Bay

floating log rafts
downstream

Kisogawa River

holding pen

Transporting Lumber Downstream

The logs sent down from the upper reaches of Kisogawa River were collected downstream in a great holding pen. There they were sorted by size, roped together into rafts, and floated out to Ise Bay.

The size of the logs was commensurate with the enormity of the castle plan; it is said that some measured more than 33 meters long by 1.5 meters in diameter at the narrower end. Such monster logs were even harder than stone blocks to transport, and a thousand men might be needed to move just one. In a fashion reminiscent of the Panama Canal project in modern times, Kisogawa River was dammed in various places to strengthen the current enough to carry the logs to the mouth of Ise Bay. There they were loaded on board ship and transported to Edo in a process that could take up to a year.

guiding logs downstream

backpacking stone

pole-and-basket

oxcart

sledge

Transport within the City

The stone and lumber offloaded at the wharves in Edo Harbor had to be delivered to the building site over the newly constructed earthen streets. The stone blocks were pulled on sledges. Atop the blocks were riders dressed in outlandish costumes who waved flags and beat drums and bells to coordinate the efforts of the vast numbers of laborers. Thousands of blocks were moved this way, some pulled by as many as three to five thousand men. Kelp was spread under the rollers to make the sledges slide more easily. Smaller blocks were loaded on oxcarts or barrows, and the gravel used for fill behind stone walls was carried by pole-and-basket (*mokko*) or by backpack.

It was rough work for rough men. Each daimyo tried to outdo his rivals in building the best walls, and the work went on day and night, keeping the new city in a perpetual uproar. Naturally fights occasionally broke out among the work crews, and the daimyo issued various laws to curb them, such as the following:

Item: Shogunal officials will be strictly obeyed.
Item: In an altercation between men of the same crew, both sides will be punished.
Item: Let there be no gossip.
Item: Fraternization between men of different domains is forbidden.
Item: Drinking on the job is prohibited.
Item: Wrestling matches are forbidden, as is going out late at night.

But such rules were hard to enforce.

Building the Stone Walls of Edo Castle

In the fourth month of 1605, when construction was reaching full swing, Ieyasu passed the office of shogun to his son Hidetada (1579–1632) and retired. The new shogun appointed Naitō Tadakiyo, Kanda Masatoshi, Tsuzuki Tamemasa, and Ishikawa Shige-tsugu as magistrates of construction, then ordered the renowned warlord and castle architect Tōdō Takatora (1556–1630) to rework the basic castle layout (called the *nawabari*). Takatora had already designed Kōriyama, Wakayama, and Kokura castles while working for the Toyotomi house and was famous for his castle plans. After the battle of Sekigahara, Takatora won the confidence of Ieyasu, and he prepared the plans for Nijō Castle in Kyoto and Fushimi Castle a few kilometers further south of it to counter the strength of Osaka Castle, built by Hideyoshi. He was now committed to making Edo Castle the greatest in the land.

Takatora assembled under him a pool of construction experts from around the country. Stonemasons who specialized in castle foundation walls were known as *anō*, after the town of that name in Ōmi Province (Shiga Prefecture). The earlier warlord Oda Nobunaga had employed them to build the great stone walls of his Azuchi Castle, the structure that revolutionized Japanese castle architecture. Among the *anō* who had worked with Takatora for the Toyotomi were those of the Tonami house, and they brought with them many of their own men from Suruga (Shizuoka Prefecture)

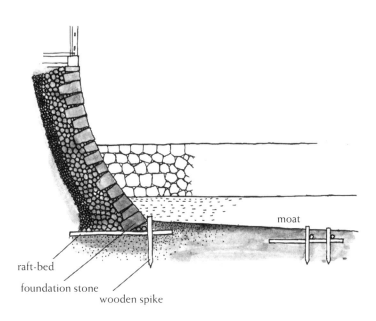

raft-bed

foundation stone

wooden spike

moat

arrow

and Mikawa (Aichi Prefecture) to work on the Edo Castle project. The various daimyo then hired their own anō to work under these foremen appointed by the shogunate, and they divided up the task of building the castle walls.

The task was complicated by the fact that part of Edo Castle was not built on bedrock but instead on marshland reclaimed from Hibiya Cove, making the walls liable to sink into the mire as they were built up. To combat this problem, rafts of pine logs were sunk into the mud, where they were fixed in place with long wooden spikes in order to support the stone above them. But this "raft-bed" technique was not foolproof, and newly built walls still often collapsed. In one case more than a hundred men working for the daimyo Asano Nagaakira were crushed to death.

Katō Kiyomasa's response when he heard of the disaster is famous. He ordered laborers to go out into Musashi Plain and bring back masses of reeds to spread over the marshland, and he then brought in children from ten to fifteen years old to play on them. Over time the reeds were trampled into a foundation. While Lord Katō's segment of the project took longer than Lord Asano's, it was strong enough to withstand an earthquake.

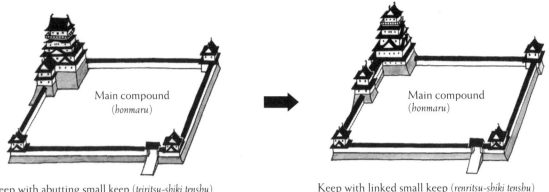

Keep with abutting small keep (*teiritsu-shiki tenshu*)   Keep with linked small keep (*renritsu-shiki tenshu*)

Designing a Keep Complex

After the stone foundation walls were completed, work could begin on the castle structures themselves. The Tokugawa house had long relied on Kihara Yoshitsugu to superintend its building projects, but for Edo Castle the Tokugawa also enlisted the services of Nakai Masakiyo (1565–1619), who learned his craft working at the ancient Hōryūji Temple in Nara and who brought with him numerous skilled craftsmen from the Kansai area.

Masakiyo had been trained by his father, who appears to have been Toyotomi Hideyoshi's master carpenter at Osaka Castle. After the defeat of the anti-Tokugawa forces at Sekigahara, he won the confidence of the Tokugawa as Tōdō Takatora had, and the two builders collaborated on the construction of Nijō and Fushimi Castles. Though Ieyasu and then his son Hidetada ruled the nation as shogun, there still remained a threat from Toyotomi Hideyoshi's son Hideyori (1593–1615), who held the mighty Osaka Castle. Nakai Masakiyo was specifically engaged because of his knowledge of Osaka Castle's design and his ability to help Edo Castle surpass it.

The ground plan of Edo Castle as laid out by Takatora was of spiral design like the city itself, with the main compound on the high ground surrounded by radiating outer compounds: the second compound, third compound, west compound, and north compound. Of all castle plans, this so-called "whirlpool design" (*kakaku-shiki*) was the most complex and difficult to attack. Atop this foundation, Masakiyo built a keep complex larger and more modern than that of Osaka Castle.

The keep complex, located in the main compound, consisted of the great keep (*daitenshu*) flanked by small keeps linked by corridors to the east, north, and west forming a square around the keep compound (*tenshumaru*). This is the so-called "encircling keeps" (*kanritsu-shiki tenshu*) design. The keep compound provided a last bastion should the main compound be breached.

Azuchi Castle of Oda Nobunaga and Osaka Castle of Toyotomi Hideyoshi had keeps with smaller towers (*yagura*) next to them in the so-called "keep with abutting small keep" design. This was before the development of larger towers—small keeps in themselves—such as those at Edo Castle. The Tokugawa stronghold with its encircling small keeps was a new technology meant to be impregnable.

Encircling keeps (*kanritsu-shiki tenshu*)

Main compound
(*honmaru*)

Keep compound
(*tenshumaru*)

Main compound
(*honmaru*)

Free-standing keep (*tanritsu-shiki tenshu*)

Building the Great Keep

The keep complex that Nakai Masakiyo designed for Edo Castle was on a scale hitherto unknown. Its construction followed that of the official and residential parts of the main compound, which were completed in the ninth month of 1606 and where Shogun Tokugawa Hidetada now lived. To the northwest, an army of workers contributed by Date Masamune (of Sendai), Uesugi Kagekatsu (of Yonezawa), Gamō Hideyuki (of Aizu), and other daimyo from Kantō and points further north were building stone foundation walls 15.8 meters high, upon which the keep complex would rest. In 1607 another tier of foundation walls 3.9 meters in height was added for the great keep.

This nearly 20-meter-tall foundation was designed to support the great keep, which itself measured 44.3 meters in height. The keep appeared to have five stories from the outside, though inside there were actually six, plus a cellar (*anagura*). The ground floor measured 33.9 meters east to west and 38.2 meters north to south, while the top floor measured 12.1 meters east to west and 16.4 meters north to south. The main compound itself was 20 meters high, meaning that the great keep towered more than 84 meters above the city. The roof tiles were of lead, to provide the best protection from the elements. It was the first test of such metal tiles; hitherto terra-cotta tiles had been the norm for castle roofs. Summer and winter, they glistened white as snow.

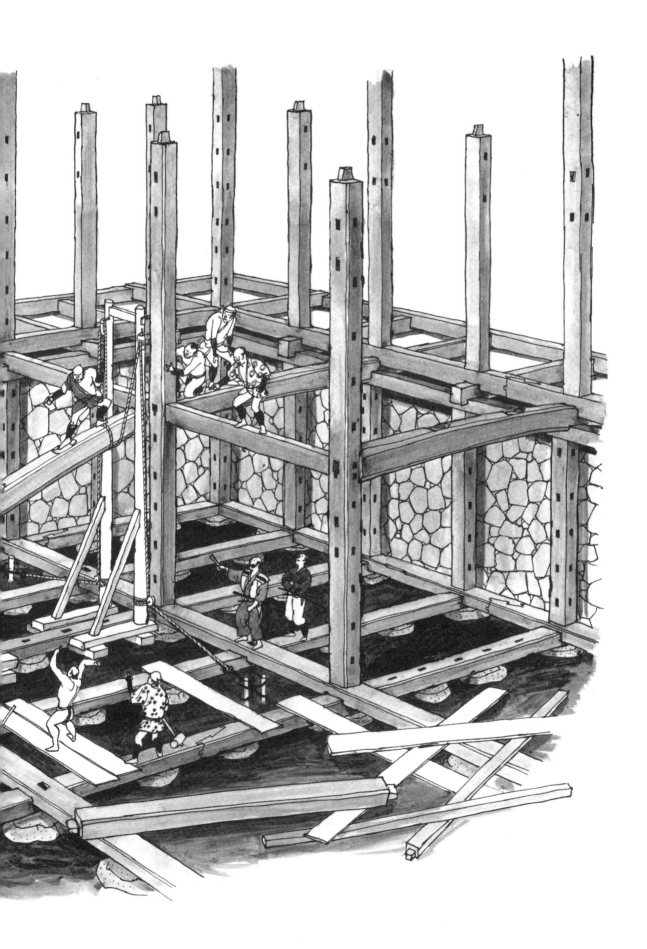

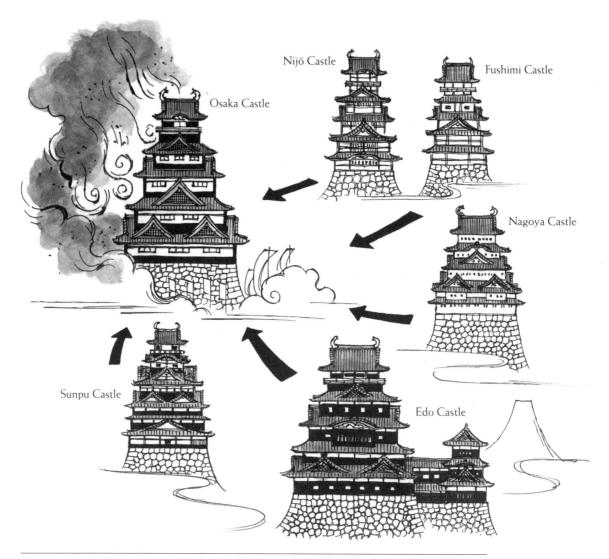

Nijō Castle

Fushimi Castle

Osaka Castle

Nagoya Castle

Sunpu Castle

Edo Castle

The Osaka Campaigns

Once Edo Castle was completed, Ieyasu began work on his own retirement castle in Sunpu, capital of Suruga Province (Shizuoka Prefecture). Initially completed at the end of 1607, it was immediately destroyed in a fire and had to be rebuilt the following year. Ieyasu followed this in 1610 with yet another castle project in Nagoya, halfway down the Tōkaidō Highroad between Edo and Osaka. Like Edo Castle, these projects were all national efforts, with ground plans by Tōdō Takatora and architectural plans by Nakai Masakiyo.

When Nagoya Castle was completed in 1614, it gave the Tokugawa five fortresses on the Tōkaidō Highroad (along with Edo, Sunpu, Nijō, and Fushimi). The shogunate was thus well prepared to oppose Toyotomi Hideyoshi's son Hideyori and his allies at Osaka Castle. Ieyasu and Hidetada initially did so in the Osaka Winter Campaign of 1614, followed shortly thereafter by the Summer Campaign of 1615, in which Osaka Castle was finally overcome. Hideyori committed suicide, and Ieyasu had his soldiers hunt down the defeated survivors, then display their heads by the thousands along the Osaka roadsides. Ieyasu was raised in a hard school, and he gave no quarter when supremacy over the nation was the prize.

The Death of Tokugawa Ieyasu

With the destruction of the Toyotomi house, the Tokugawa faced no further opposition to their regime. This marked the end of the civil wars that had plagued the country since the mid-16th century and the beginning of the long Pax Tokugawa.

In the fourth month of the following year, 1616, Ieyasu died at age 74 in his castle at Sunpu, having lived just long enough to see the final defeat of his foes and the perpetuation of his own house. In accordance with his last will and testament, he was buried on Kunōzan Mountain, only to be moved later to Tōshōgū Shrine in Nikkō. The shrine took its name from Ieyasu's posthumous title, Tōshō Daigongen ("Illuminator of the East, Great Buddha Incarnate").

A Tōshōgū Shrine to his memory was also built on Momijiyama Hill in Edo Castle, as if to allow his spirit to stand quiet watch over his growing city.

Expanding the Castle Periphery

With the advent of peace, Edo Castle had to adapt to a new, non-bellicose function. Together with being the residence of the shogun, it would have to be redesigned to accommodate more pervasive administrative uses. To effect this, Hidetada decided to exploit the city's spiral plan by expanding the canal system to redefine the castle periphery.

The shogunate began the project at the northeast, levelling part of Kandayama Hill and changing the course of Hirakawa River to connect with Sumidagawa River. This enormous feat of engineering was accomplished in the autumn of 1620. The old

Ochanomizu

outer canal, which included Hirakawa Ōmagari, Iidabashi, Kudanshita, Kandabashi, and Nihonbashi, now became the inner canal. The new outer canal, named Kanda-gawa River, included Koishikawa, Ochanomizu, Sujikaibashi, and Asakusabashi. This expansion not only increased the area of the castle but also ended the flooding of Hirakawa River, which had brought considerable suffering to the residents of the Honchō area. The earth taken from Kandayama Hill, furthermore, was used to fill in more of Hibiya Cove, which allowed further expansion of the city to the southeast. And the southern heights now demarcated by Kandagawa River were opened up to warriors from Sunpu, the capital of Suruga Province, and renamed Surugadai Heights. The Kandayama project thus killed not just two but four birds with one stone.

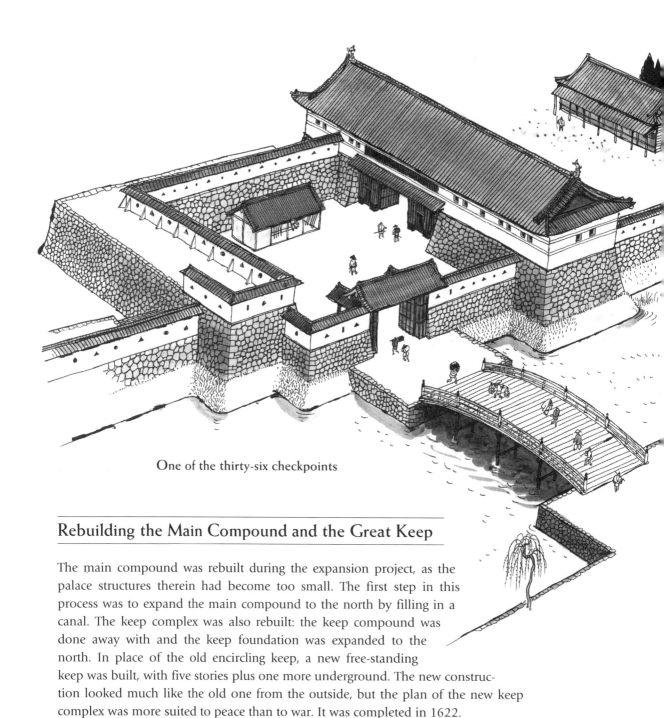

One of the thirty-six checkpoints

Rebuilding the Main Compound and the Great Keep

The main compound was rebuilt during the expansion project, as the palace structures therein had become too small. The first step in this process was to expand the main compound to the north by filling in a canal. The keep complex was also rebuilt: the keep compound was done away with and the keep foundation was expanded to the north. In place of the old encircling keep, a new free-standing keep was built, with five stories plus one more underground. The new construction looked much like the old one from the outside, but the plan of the new keep complex was more suited to peace than to war. It was completed in 1622.

In the seventh month of the following year, Hidetada passed on the office of shogun to his eldest son Iemitsu (1604–51) and retired to a residence in the west compound. Moving into the new main compound, the new shogun began work on a

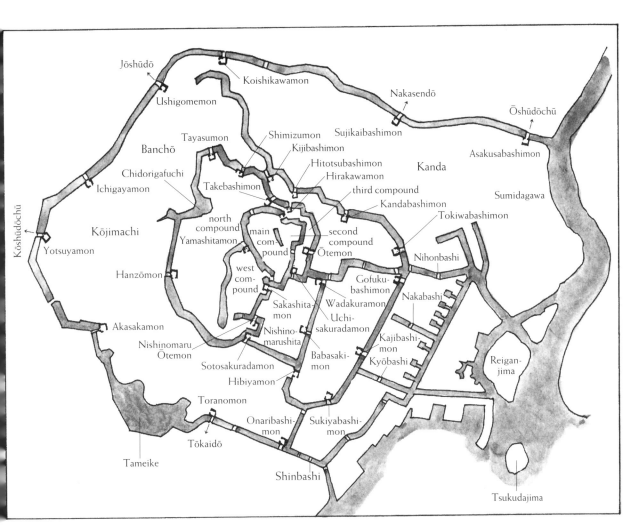

Jōshūdō

Koishikawamon

Ushigomemon

Nakasendō

Ōshūdōchū

Tayasumon

Shimizumon

Sujikaibashimon

Banchō

Kijibashimon

Asakusabashimon

Chidorigafuchi

Hitotsubashimon

Kanda

Ichigayamon

Takebashimon

Hirakawamon

Kōshūdōchū

north
compound

third compound

Sumidagawa

Kōjimachi

Yamashitamon

main
com-
pound

second
compound

Kandabashimon

Yotsuyamon

Tokiwabashimon

Hanzōmon

west
com-
pound

Ōtemon

Nihonbashi

Gofuku-
bashimon

Nakabashi

Akasakamon

Sakashita-
mon

Wadakuramon

Uchi-
sakuradamon

Nishino-
marushita

Kajibashi-
mon

Reigan-
jima

Nishinomaru
Ōtemon

Babasaki-
mon

Kyōbashi

Sotosakuradamon

Hibiyamon

Toranomon

Onaribashi-
mon

Sukiyabashi-
mon

Tōkaidō

Tameike

Shinbashi

Tsukudajima

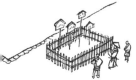

second complex in the second compound that would include a teahouse and a spacious garden. This second complex, finished in 1630, was laid out by the master designer Kobori Enshū (1579–1647) and was even more splendid than the princely Katsura Detached Palace in Kyoto, begun in the early 17th century and extant, which also reflects Enshū's style.

The spiral system of canals was eventually punctuated at intervals by thirty-two massive, fortified castle gates called checkpoints (*mitsuke*). They were figuratively referred to as "the thirty-six checkpoints," after the famous "thirty-six poets" in earlier times. Of these, the most important were the "Five Doors to Edo" (*Edo gokō*): Toranomon Gate for the Tōkaidō, Yotsuyamon Gate for the Kōshūdōchū, Ushigomemon Gate for the Jōshūdō, Sujikaibashimon Gate for the Nakasendō, and Asakusabashimon Gate for the Ōshūdōchū highroads. Shogunal officials manned each one and checked all traffic in and out of the city to keep the peace.

Completing the New Outer Canal and a Third Great Keep

Hidetada died in 1632, leaving his son Iemitsu to oversee the building of the last canal link to the northwest of the castle that would create a new unbroken canal periphery. This last link, begun in 1635, connected Tameike Pond, Akasaka, Yotsuya, Ichigaya, and Ushigome with Kanadagawa River, the northeast peripheral canal finished earlier by Hidetada. When completed, the new perimeter of Edo Castle reached far beyond that of Ieyasu's original fortress.

Iemitsu also carried out yet another rebuilding of the main compound, appointing Sakai Tadakatsu (1587–1662) as the general magistrate (*sōbugyō*) for the project, which began in 1637. The best carpenters, stonemasons, plasterers, metalworkers, lacquerers, and painters were brought in to work under a head carpenter from Edo, Kihara Yoshihisa, and another from Kyoto, Nakai Masazumi, and further enlarge and ornament the great keep, official and residence halls, and the Tōshōgū Shrine to Ieyasu's memory. When these projects were completed, they proved altogether too magnificent for even Iemitsu himself, who ordered them toned down.

The building project took longer than expected, not only because of a fire in the castle at one point but also because of the shogunate's involvement in the suppression of an uprising in 1637–38 of thousands of peasants in Shimabara and Amakusa in Kyushu, who were protesting harsh local government and in particular the official repression of the Christian faith, which claimed many adherents in the area. But construction was finally completed in the fourth month of 1640, fifty years after work had first begun on the castle.

Edo Castle's Main Compound

With the completion of the new outer canal, the old outer bastion of the castle was now the inner, consisting of the main compound and its great keep together with the second compound, third compound, west compound, and north compound, all expanding outward in a clockwise spiral. At nearly two square kilometers in area, the inner bastion alone equalled the average area covered by entire castle towns in the rest of the country. Its enormous scale made clear the fortress's national preeminence. Housed within the inner bastion of the castle were a huge number of structures, including not only the great keep and palace buildings but twenty-one subsidiary towers, twenty-eight *tamon* (as "long house" tenements within the inner bastion were called), ninety-nine gates, and almost innumerable reception and residence halls and storehouses.

The main compound included a dense maze of palace structures. To reach them, one entered the inner bastion via the Ōtemon Gate at the east of the third compound and then continued on through the Chūjakumon Gate at the main compound's southeast end.

The palace buildings were divided into three main groups: the outer complex

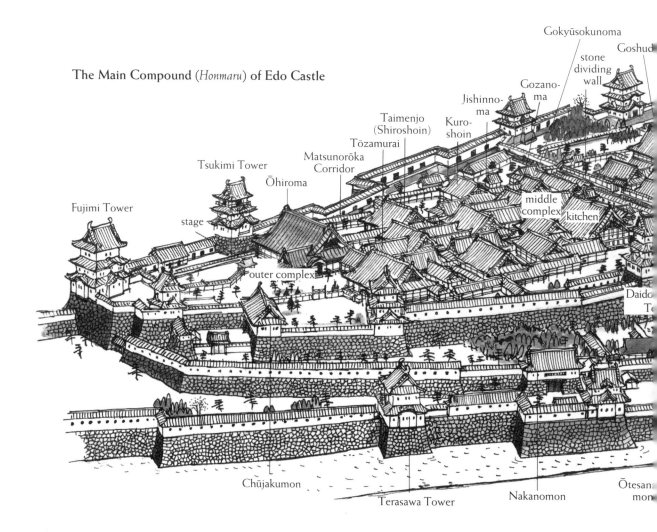

The Main Compound (*Honmaru*) of Edo Castle

(*omote*), middle complex (*nakaoku*), and inner complex (*oku*). The outer complex was where the official business of the shogunate was conducted. At its heart was the Ōhiroma (Great Hall), familiarly known as the "Thousand-Mat Hall" (Senjōjiki). Included as well were the enormous Shiroshoin (White Shoin) and Kuroshoin (Black Shoin) audience halls, the name *shoin* having originally meant "study hall" but later being more generally applied. They were profusely decorated, boasting fittings by famous carvers like Kōra Bungo and Heinouchi Ōsumi and screens of gold and polychrome by renowned painters like Kanō Tan'yū. The riot of color rivalled that of Tōshōgū Shrine in Nikkō, famous today for its opulence.

The middle complex of the main compound was the shogunal residence. Its main structures were the Gozanoma and Gokyūsokunoma Halls, along with a strongly reinforced structure called Earthquake Hall (Jishinnoma). There was in addition a huge kitchen and many rooms for the shogun's warrior servants.

The inner complex was reserved for the shogun's wife and his other consorts. This area was sectioned off by a stone wall, and only women were allowed within. Together with the Goshuden, the chambers of the shogun's wife, were countless rooms for her maids, the whole area being so large that it was often called "the great interior" (*ōoku*).

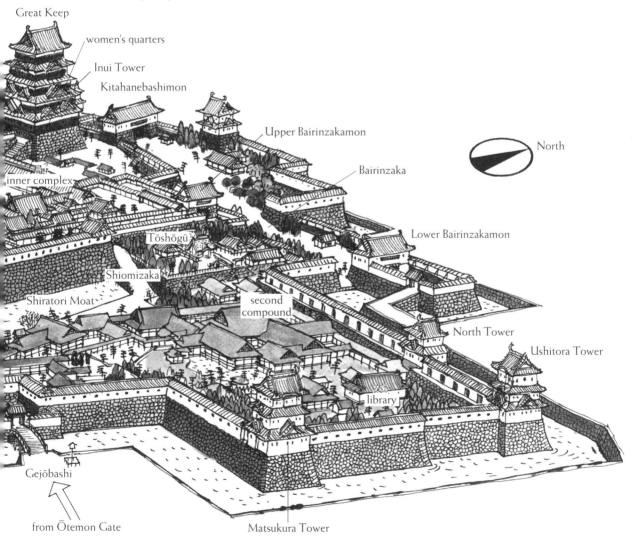

Great Keep

women's quarters

Inui Tower

Kitahanebashimon

Upper Bairinzakamon

North

inner complex

Bairinzaka

Tōshōgū

Lower Bairinzakamon

Shiomizaka

Shiratori Moat

second compound

North Tower

Ushitora Tower

library

Gejōbashi

from Ōtemon Gate

Matsukura Tower

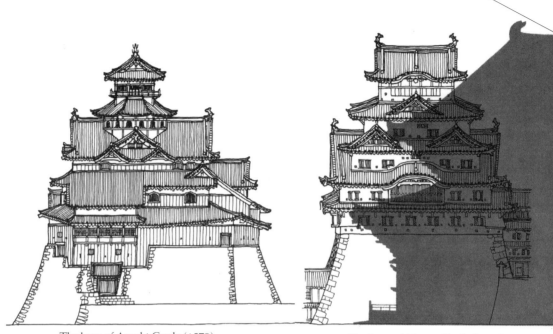

The keep of Azuchi Castle (1579)

The keep of Himeji Castle (1609)

1582　Oda Nobunaga is assassinated at Honnōji Temple
1583　Toyotomi Hideyoshi begins building Osaka Castle
1598　Hideyoshi dies
1600　Battle of Sekigahara
1603　Tokugawa Ieyasu founds the Edo (Tokugawa) Shogunate

Early watchtower style　　　➡　　　Late watchtower style

The Development of the Castle Keep

The great keep that rose up behind the inner complex, at the northwest corner of the main compound, was the tallest building in Japanese history. As described earlier, it was originally built in Ieyasu's time on the "encircling keep" plan, then rebuilt by Hidetada as a free-standing structure. It was rebuilt a third time by Iemitsu, remaining free-standing but being even further enlarged.

The history of the castle keep in Japan begins with Azuchi Castle of Oda Nobunaga. Nobunaga rose to preeminence among the warring daimyo lords in the latter 16th century, and to demonstrate in architectural terms his new authority, he set out to construct a castle that would exceed in height the largest building in the land, the Great Buddha Hall (Daibutsuden) of Tōdaiji Temple in Nara (which even today remains the largest wooden building on earth). The completed keep turned out to be about equal in height to the Tōdaiji structure, which remained the benchmark for Hideyoshi and Ieyasu as well. But Iemitsu's third Edo Castle keep surpassed the Great Buddha Hall and became the tallest structure in the country. Its design, too, was the most advanced.

The keep of Azuchi Castle, built in 1579, was designed in the "watchtower style" (*bōrōgata*), which consisted of a tower of three external stories topped by a two-story cupola. This two-part design was vulnerable to earthquakes and typhoons. Hideyoshi's

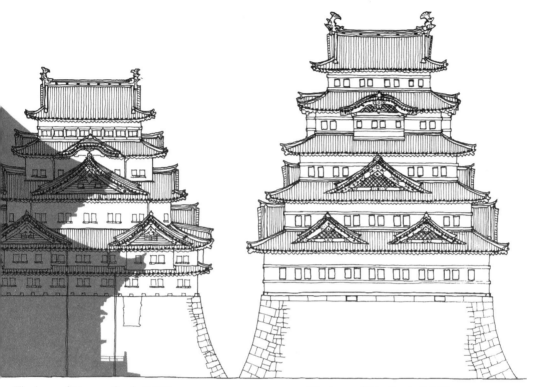

The keep of Nagoya Castle (1612)   The keep of Edo Castle (1638)

1615 The Toyotomi house is destroyed in the Osaka Summer Campaign   1657 Edo Castle burns in the great
1615 The "one domain, one castle" law is promulgated   Meireki fire; the keep is not
1616 Ieyasu dies   rebuilt
1632 Tokugawa Hidetada dies

Early multistory tower style      Late multistory tower style

Fushimi Castle keep was also of the watchtower design and was in fact destroyed in an earthquake. Records say that Hideyoshi himself barely escaped with his life.

Keep designs improved thereafter so that they rose from bottom to top as a single, unified structure, in a so-called "multistory tower style" (*sōtōgata*). The keep of Himeji, probably Japan's most famous extant castle, still retains a later version of the watchtower style, while that of Nagoya Castle, built only three years later in 1612, used the multistory tower design (it was destroyed in the Second World War and a replica stands today). The keep of Iemitsu's Edo Castle was a further refinement of that later style, designed so that each of its four facades presented an imposing appearance. This was referred to as a "universal front" (*happō shōmen*) design.

The most advanced techniques were employed to make Edo Castle impervious to the elements and impregnable to hostile forces. Though the core of the structure was made of wood, the thick walls were of wattle-and-daub construction and covered with plaster. The roof tiles and parts of the walls of its third great keep were made not of lead but of copper, giving the structure a green cast and making it highly fire-resistant, if not entirely fireproof (as later events would prove). Gracing both ends of the roof ridge were *shachihoko*—finials shaped as mythical, dolphin-like fish—as was a common practice for castle keeps. The enormous tower thus became a symbol of the strength and majesty of the regime that erected it.

The Daimyo Kōji District

Many of the *fudai* and *tozama* daimyo lived in Daimyo Kōji at the east of the inner bastion, and each vied with the others to build mansions of surpassing splendor. They boasted "all-day gates" (*higurashimon*) with such riveting sculpture and polychromy that a viewer might stare till the sun set and still not take in all the details. A particularly famous example of such gates can still be seen at the Tōshōgū Shrine dedicated to Ieyasu at Nikkō, built by his grandson Iemitsu. One of the most magnificent "all-day gates" was that of Katō Kiyomasa. 19.7 meters wide, it sported dragon, tiger, and even rhinocerous sculptures together with gold leaf that shone bright enough to make it almost an "all-night gate" as well.

Such gates were built to advertise the power of the great daimyo whose domains might encompass entire provinces. The gates of such mansions were next in scale only to Ōtemon Gate of Edo Castle. Tenements (*nagaya*) for retainers ringed the area inside, and two-story towers at the corners kept watch. The lords also built special entrances, called "processional gates" (*onarimon*), and sumptuous "processional palaces" (*onari goten*) for entertaining the shogun when he called.

The Kōrakuen Garden of the Lower
Mansion of the Mito Domain

Hundred-ken Tenement

Cherry Equestrian Field

Lapis Teahouse

Lotus Pond

Maruya Teahouse

Saigyōdō Hall

Benten Shrine

Hōraijima
Island

Daisensui
Pond

Water Stage

Long Bridge

Fukurokudō Hall

Chinese Gate

Warrior Mansions

Daimyo, as noted previously, were obliged by the system of alternate attendance to divide their time between Edo and their home domains, leaving their families in the capital as de facto hostages. They owned not one but three mansions in Edo: an "upper mansion" (*kamiyashiki*), a "middle mansion" (*nakayashiki*), and a "lower mansion" (*shimoyashiki*). The upper mansions in Daimyo Kōji, within the castle's inner bastion, were convenient for their owners to report for service to their shogunal

Kiyomizu Kannondō Hall

Tsujidō Gazebo

jindō Hall

Octagon Hall

North

Chinese-style stone bridge

Hakorōka Corridor

plum trees

kitchen

Eight-Fold Bridge

Shoin

wooden gate

irises

wisteria trellis

stage

New Teahouse

overlord. The middle mansions, located within the outer canal, were subsidiary structures where wives and children lived.

Lower mansions were villas built outside the central part of the city, and they normally included spacious gardens. One that remains today is Kōrakuen Garden (now Kōrakuen Park), originally part of the lower mansion of the lord of the Mito domain, one of the three branches of the Tokugawa house. Designed according to Chinese landscape principles, it was furnished with bridges and numerous cottages and was famous for its size, which exceeded even that of the garden in the second compound of Edo Castle. The shogun himself sometimes came to visit.

The lower mansions were also sometimes referred to as "storehouse mansions" (*kurayashiki*), as it was in these mansions near Edo Harbor that goods from the lords' domains were offloaded and stored.

Beyond the outer canal stood the residences of lower-ranking warriors (*hanshi*). Most were tenements, and like today's apartment blocks they held a number of families. Such buildings were very plain and simple, a world away from the mansions of the great lords.

waystation

relay horse

courier

League Markers and Waystations

It was in 1604 that the shogunate officially designated the five great highroads: the Tōkaidō, Nakasendō, Kōshūdōchū, Ōshūdōchū, and Nikkōdōchū, all of which originated at Nihonbashi in Edo. It further stipulated that every league (*ri*, approximately four kilometers) would be indicated by a marker placed on a mound planted with a large tree such as a hackberry or pine.

Waystations were also established to aid travellers or teamsters on official shogunal business. Such waystations were vital for the operation of the relay system the shogunate devised. Each station kept a fixed number of relay horses (*tenma*) and teamsters which would relay goods from their station to the next on the highroad, in

notice boards

league marker

a process known as *yadotsugi* (station to station). Particularly well known were the 53 stations of the Tōkaidō, from Nihonbashi in Edo, past Mount Fuji, and west to the Great Sanjō Bridge (Sanjō Ōhashi) in Kyoto. These stations were depicted in series of woodblock prints by Katsushika Hokusai (1760–1849) and Andō Hiroshige (1797–1858).

In Edo proper, the important waystations were Ōdenmachō, Minami Denmachō, and Kodenmachō. The first two handled the freight on the five highroads, and the last, that for the immediate Edo area. In this age before the telephone and telegraph, official messages were carried by couriers (*hikyaku*, lit., "flying feet"). These were of three kinds, the "relay couriers" (*tsugihikyaku*) for the shogunate, "daimyo couriers" (*daimyō hikyaku*) for the great lords, and "town couriers" (*machi hikyaku*) for general use. A courier carried letters, money, or small packages on a pole over his shoulder. It was faster than it might sound—a package could be carried from Edo to Kyoto in 90 hours, or 60 in an emergency.

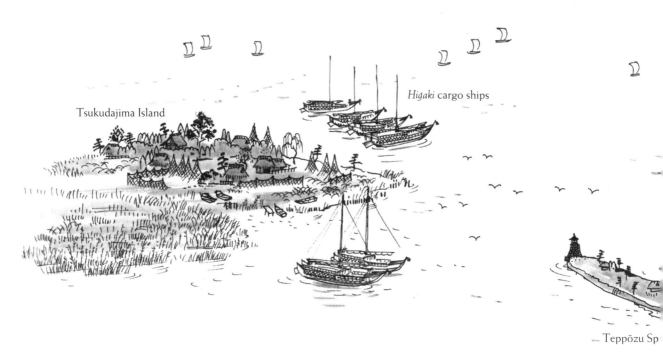

Tsukudajima Island

Higaki cargo ships

Teppōzu Sp

Edo Harbor

Because of the mandated system of alternate attendance
in Edo for all daimyo and their enormous retinues, the city
became the consumer capital of the country. Initially the Edo
infrastructure was insufficient to support the burgeoning population, and staples had to be imported from Kyoto and Osaka. These so-
called "goods that came down" (*kudarimono*) from the west to Edo via the Tōkaidō
teamster stations were highly valued by the new citizens of the military capital. Local
goods that did not "come down" were considered inferior. Particularly esteemed of
such kudarimono were "capital sake," "capital oil," "capital rice," "capital soy sauce,"
"capital candles," and "capital umbrellas."

So great was the demand for such items that it soon proved more profitable and
efficient to transport them not by land but by sea, in large cargo ships (*kaisen*). The
most important of these were the *higaki* cargo ships, famous for the diamond-shaped
latticework on their gunwales. They are said to have first been used in 1619 by a resident of Sakai, a trading city close to Osaka, to ship to Edo cotton, oil, sake, soy sauce,
and vinegar. Every year, such ships would vie with each other to bring the season's
first cotton to Edo, for the quicker the delivery, the higher the price.

Arriving in Edo Harbor, cargo vessels from around the country anchored at Teppōzu
Spit. There the cargo was offloaded onto lighters (*setoribune*) that would navigate the
city's canals and bring the goods to market.

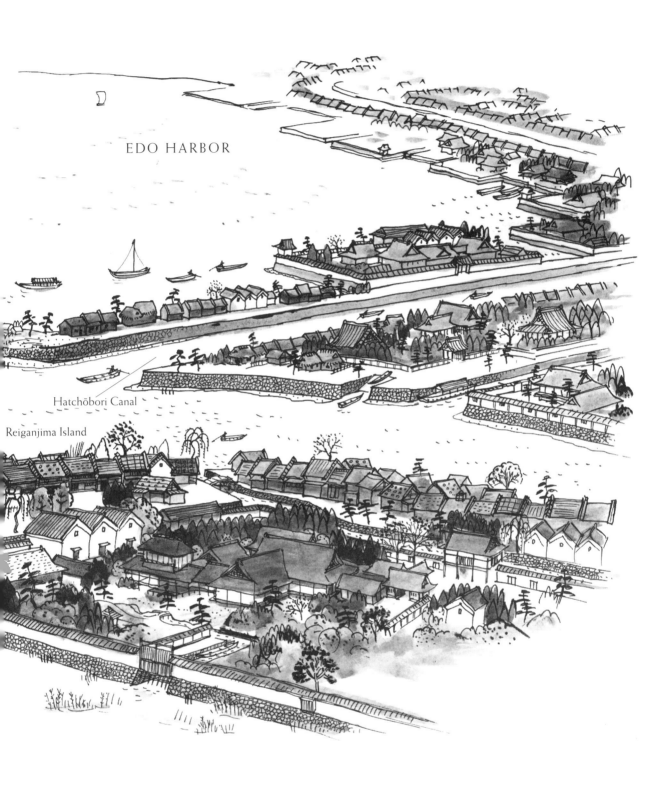

EDO HARBOR

Hatchōbori Canal

Reiganjima Island

The Fish Market

When Tokugawa Ieyasu first arrived in Edo, he brought with him fishermen from the town of Tsukudamura in Settsu Province (Osaka Prefecture). He designated the lagoons of Teppōzu Spit for their use and put them in charge of supplying the new city with fish. The fishermen built an island there, which they named Tsukudajima after their home town. This was the beginning of the famous Tsukudajima fishing industry. In exchange for fishing rights in Edo Harbor, they were required to provide for the shogun's table.

What was left from the shogunal kitchens was sold on the open market, which was located on the east riverbank at the north end of Nihonbashi Bridge, a place called Ōfunechō, or simply the Nihonbashi Fish Market. The buying and selling was fast and furious, and the riverbank became famous as one of the most bustling parts of the city, with stores lining the streets, each selling produce from the sea. They displayed their wares on large tables, or kept their fish and shellfish alive in barrels of sea water.

The streets rang with the calls of tradesmen, some of whom sold their wares from baskets slung from poles across their shoulders. One such fishmonger was Isshin Tasuke, who purveyed to the shogunal bannerman Ōkubo Hikozaemon (1560–1639). Frank and big-hearted, he was a typical "child of Edo" or *Edokko*, and for years after his death he was featured in stories and even a kabuki play.

The Water Supply

The high ground of Edo was dominated by warrior districts. Townspeople, by contrast, lived in the low areas, much of it landfill near Edo Harbor, and wells sunk there yielded only saltwater. Ieyasu's first plan for Edo had anticipated this problem and, it will be recalled, provided for the building of the Kanda and the Akasaka Tameike water systems to supply fresh water to the town. But as the population grew, these proved insufficient and new sources had to be found.

It was therefore decided to expand the Kanda system by drawing from Inokashira Pond, located further out from the city than the Kanda system's initial source, Koishikawa Marsh. Water would be fed in along the way from Zenpukujiike and Myōshōjiike ponds. Koishikawa River was diverted so as to flow by Yushima and Kandadai Heights to Ogawamachi. Thereafter, when work was begun on Kandagawa River, that river was spanned by an aqueduct (*suidōbashi*) that brought the water into the city, where it was further directed into a network of buried wooden pipes to provide water to the downtown area.

But despite these projects, the water supply could not keep up with demand, so in 1653 the Akasaka Tameike water system was closed and construction begun on the Tamagawa water system, a far larger complex. It brought in water from the Tamagawa River at Hamura, passing 29 settlements along its 52 kilometer course, including Kawasaki, Koganei, Tanashi, Kichijōji, Kugayama, Takaido, Daita, Yoyogi, Tsunohazu, and Sendagaya. When it reached Yotsuya Ōkido it went underground to Yotsuyamon Gate, where it divided into three routes.

The first went to Edo Castle, the second to the Kōjimachi area, and the third from the Yotsuya area down Kinokunizaka slope, and east of Tameike to Toranomon, then Shiba, Tsukiji, Hatchōbori, and Kyōbashi.

Drinking water was thus provided to the whole city via wooden pipes, which at intervals were fitted with bamboo conduits (*yobihi*) feeding wells from which water was drawn up in buckets. This water was strictly for drinking, and other uses were prohibited. Water for other purposes, like washing clothes, came from wells connected to the city's canals.

Aqueduct over Kandagawa River

Houses of the Townspeople

The townspeople, who lived in residential blocks (*chō*), were overseen by three city aldermen (*machidoshiyori*), who in turn reported to two city magistrates (*machi bugyō*) of the warrior class. The earliest of these aldermen, Naraya Ichiemon and Taruya Tōzaemon, were appointed from among the townspeople in 1590, the year of Ieyasu's installation in the city. A third, Kitamura Yahei, was added two years later. All three came from Ieyasu's old domain and were provided with official residences (*oyakusho*) in the First (Itchōme), Second (Nichōme), and Third (Sanchōme) sub-districts of Honchō.

The aldermen, the highest-placed townspeople in the government, were in turn served by neighborhood headmen (*nanushi*). Many of these headmen had resided in the area before Ieyasu's arrival, and were known as "pioneer headmen" (*kusawake nanushi*). Others, who had been active in the founding of the shogunate, were called "old-city headmen" (*kochō nanushi*). The headmen, who commanded great respect, generally oversaw five to eight blocks apiece.

The houses of the first townspeople were apparently roofed with straw. Wood shingles were substituted after a fire broke out in Surugachō in 1601 that destroyed the city. Edo was at that time still a simple country village by comparison to Kyoto, where nearly all the city's houses were shingle-roofed two-story structures. When Takiyama Yajibei tiled the front side of his roof, he thereby earned considerable notoriety and the nickname "Half-tiled Yajibei." It was not until the time of Tokugawa Iemitsu, the third shogun, that Edo became as prosperous as the old capital, with two-story tile-roofed structures becoming the norm and even three-story houses appearing at the block corners. Soon the number of blocks reached three hundred.

carpenters

sawyer

plasterers

tatami makers

smiths

founders

Artisan Districts

In the beginning of the city's development, the townspeople's areas were maintained gratis by the shogunate. In exchange, the residents had to perform various services for the military government. It was to that end that the shogunate required that all those of the same occupation live in the same general area. For example, indigo dyers (*aizomeya*) lived in Kanda Kon'yachō, Minami Kon'yachō, Nishi Kon'yachō, and Kita Kon'yachō; carpenters (*daiku*) in Moto Daikuchō, Minami Daikuchō, Kanda Yokodaiku (Banjō)chō, and Tate Daikuchō; smiths (*kaji*) in Kanda Kajichō, Minami

chandler

cooper

cypress woodworkers

indigo dyers

scabbard maker

lacquerer

Kajichō, and Sakurada Kajichō; plasterers (*sakan*) in Kanda Shirokabechō; sawyers (*kobiki*) in Ogachō; tatami makers (*tatamiya*) in Tatamichō; founders (*imoji*) in Kanda Nabechō; gunsmiths (*teppōshō*) in Teppōchō; and scabbard-makers (*sayashi*) in Minami-sayachō.

These districts had their own occupational headmen, who received the orders of the shogunate and farmed them out to their subordinates. Those particularly skilled at their trades were designated "purveyors to the shogunate" (*goyōtashi shokunin*) and afforded official marks of esteem, including the right to wear a sword.

The Edo Cityscape

Activity in the townspeople's districts began at dawn. The time of day was indicated by a bell (*toki no kane*) that was originally installed in the castle proper. It rang at six in the morning (*ake mutsu*) and six in the evening (*kure mutsu*). But the bell proved too noisy for its proximity to the shogunal living quarters, and so it was moved to Honkokuchō Sanchōme in Nihonbashi, where it marked time in *ittoki* intervals equivalent to two modern hours. Eventually the city grew so large that nine bells

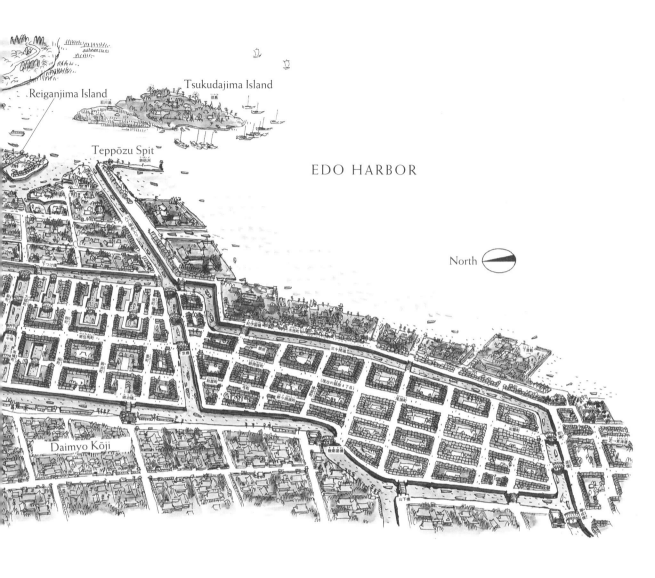

Reiganjima Island

Tsukudajima Island

Teppōzu Spit

EDO HARBOR

North

Daimyo Kōji

were set up in various places. Temples like Ueno's Kan'eiji and Asakusa's Sensōji had bells as well. The sound was immortalized by Bashō in this springtime verse, which implies the cherries bloom so thickly that from his cottage in Fukagawa he cannot tell where the sound is coming from:

Clouds of blossoms—
is that bell Ueno's?
Akasaka's?

Merchant Districts

As Edo's prosperity grew to rival and then exceed that of Kyoto, merchants began to flock there from all parts of the country, in particular Ise (Mie Prefecture), Ōmi (Shiga Prefecture), and Kyoto itself. Ise was a cotton-producing region, and Ise merchants began to make use of their cargo ships for cotton to transport various other products from central Honshū, including paper, household utensils, lamp oil, and tea. Signs bearing the name Iseya (House of Ise) cropped up all over the city, to the point where a popular alliterative ditty held that the three most common things in Edo were "Iseya shops, Inari shrines, and dog shit" (*Iseya, Inari ni, inu no kuso*).

But the concerns dealing in the most expensive items still tended to come from Kyoto and Osaka. Products acquired from around the country were stocked in the main stores (*hontana*) in Kyoto and Osaka, then sent to Edo outlets, where they were sold in quantity. The largest of these outlets, called Edodana, tended to be located in Ōdenmachō, a major teamster center where goods entered the city.

firebell

police station

wooden gate

notice boards

Gates, Watchmen, and Notice Boards

Each block (*chō*) of houses built along the expanding spiral of canals was separated from the next by a street entered through a wooden gate (*kido*). Next to each entrance was a "wooden-gate station" (*kido ban'ya*). The watchman, a member of the local community, was known familiarly as "Watchman Tarō" (Ban Tarō), Tarō being a common given name. People were free to come and go during daylight hours, but the gate was closed at ten o'clock each night to help keep the peace. This had been particularly important in Edo's rough-and-ready early years, when fights and even murders were common and a samurai might occasionally test his sword on a passerby.

The shogunate was hard pressed to keep order, and in 1628 it established "corner

rainwater for firefighting

stations" (*tsuji bansho*) in the warrior districts and "police stations" (*jishin ban'ya*) in the townspeople's areas, generally one per block, set up at the wooden gates. They were like the "wooden-gate stations" except that they dispatched peace officers, again appointed from the local communities, on rounds throughout the neighborhoods to suppress crime and violence. These officers also manned the fire lookout towers (*hinomiyagura*) that stood nearby.

Residents in each block were organized into "five-family groups" (*goningumi*), and shogunal orders were passed down to them via the hierarchy of city magistrates, city aldermen, and neighborhood headmen. Instrumental in this process were the notice boards (*kōsatsu*) that stood in conspicuous locations. The first such board was located at the south end of Nihonbashi Bridge, and they later proliferated to several dozen.

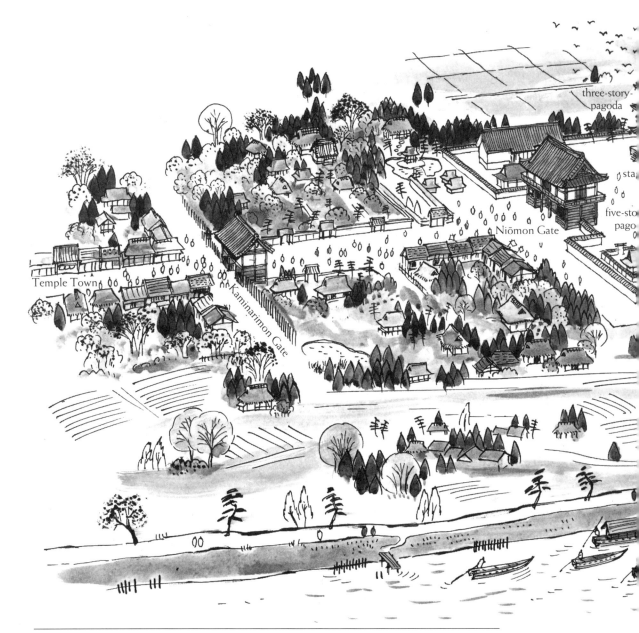

three-story-pagoda

$\oint$ sta.

five-sto
pago

Niōmon Gate

Temple Town

Kaminarimon Gate

A Bustling Religious District—Sensōji Temple

The growth of townspeople's districts brought corresponding prosperity to areas set aside for Shinto shrines and Buddhist temples. Such religious districts were located at busy transit points outside the city's outer canal. Three that were particularly famous were Zōjōji Temple for the Tōkaidō, Kan'eiji for the Nakasendō, and Sensōji (or Asakusa Kannon) for the Ōshūdōchū.

Sensōji, the oldest, had stood near the shore of Sumidagawa River for centuries. Soon after Ieyasu entered the city, he designated this ancient Tendai Buddhist establishment a tutelary temple of the Tokugawa house. When Senju Ōhashi Bridge was built over Arakawa River, at the start of the Ōshūdōchū, Sensōji's "temple town" (*monzenmachi*, lit., "town outside the temple gate") became the point of entry into Edo from the north and enjoyed unprecedented prosperity.

But this was low ground, and from time to time Arakawa River flooded, bringing

Tōshōgū Shrine

Sanja Gongen Shrine

bell tower

main hall

SUMIDAGAWA RIVER

misery to the locals. The shogunate therefore constructed in 1621 a massive levee to the northeast of Sensōji. All the daimyo in the land were mobilized to help build it, and thus it was called Nihonzutsumi or "Japan Levee." Thousands flocked to Sensōji and its environs, now completely safe, to worship and perhaps enjoy boating on the river. Passing through the town, one arrived first at Kaminarimon ("Thunder Gate") and then Niōmon ("Benevolent Kings Gate"), the entrance to the inner complex of temple halls, which included a three-story pagoda to the left, a five-story one to the right, and beyond them in the center the main hall with a stage in front. There one prayed to the Bodhisattva Kannon, and perhaps then went further back to the left to pay one's respects at Tōshōgū Shrine, dedicated to the spirit of Ieyasu. One might also visit the Three Shrines (Sanja) within the temple complex. The Sanja Festival (*Sanja matsuri*) connected with the Sensōji shrines, held on the 17th and 18th of the third month (by the lunar calendar), was numbered among the three great festivals of the city, along with the Sannōsha and Kanda festivals.

Five-Story Pagoda

Tōshōgū Shrine

Kanshōin Hall

bell tower

Yakushidō Hall

Monjudō Hall

Spook Lantern

Great Buddha

Niōmon Gate

Yanakamichi Road

Shinobazunoike Pond

Bentenjima Island

Kan'eiji Temple in Ueno

The next oldest temple after Sensōji to be built in Edo was Zōjōji, of the Pure Land (Jōdo) Buddhist sect. Since that denomination had been particularly popular in the Tokugawa house's original province of Mikawa, the shogunate chose Zōjōji as another of its tutelary temples and the place for the veneration of the house ancestors. Then in 1592, the shogunate moved another Pure Land temple, Seiganji, to Kanda, and that sect went on to be the most popular in the shogun's capital. In 1624, the shogunate decided to build another Tendai temple (the sect of Sensōji) in Ueno, northeast

Jōgyōdō Hall

Hokkedō Hall

...zō Repository

Tahōtō Pagoda

Honbō

Sanjūban Jinja Shrine

Kiyomizu Kannondō Hall

of the castle. The northeast, a city's "demon gate" (*kimon*), was traditionally held to be vulnerable to malign spirits, and this area accordingly needed particular divine protection. It was the same belief that had spurred the construction of the great Tendai temple Enryakuji atop Mount Hiei, to the northeast of the city of Kyoto. To mark its similarity of function with its ancient Kyoto counterpart, the new temple was given the formal prefix Tōeizan, "Hiei of the East."

The designers of the expansive compound on Ueno Hill marked its southern entryway with Niōmon Gate and its statues of the two "Benevolent Kings" (Niō) to either side of the gate's doors. Immediately to the left inside the gate they placed a huge statue of a seated Buddha, modeled on those in the great Buddha halls in Nara and Kyoto. Directly across from the Buddha to the other side of the gate they gave another nod to ancient tradition, Kiyomizu Kannondō, based on Kyoto's Kiyomizudera Temple. Behind Niōmon Gate they located a stone lantern so huge it seemed supernatural, and was therefore named "Spook Lantern" (Obakedōrō), and to its left they erected a five-story pagoda and a Tōshōgū Shrine. Further into the precinct were placed Tahōtō Pagoda to the right and Rinzō Repository and a bell tower to the left. And finally at the north end were built a pair of halls, Jōgyōdō to the left and Hokkedō to the right, linked by a bridge spanning the temple's axial road; they were nicknamed the "carrying-pole halls" (*ninai-dō*) for their resemblance to a carrying pole with bundles at both ends.

These edifices were decorated with dragons that legend holds were carved by Hidari Jingorō, to whom are also attributed the magnificent carvings of the shogunal mausoleum at Nikkō. The dragons were so realistic they were said to come alive at night and sneak down to Shinobazunoike Pond to slake their thirst. The pond, too, had an earlier precedent in Kyoto's Lake Biwa, east of Mount Hiei. The relationship was made closer still when in 1642 Bentenjima Island was added, modelled on Lake Biwa's Chikubushima Island. The island was eventually linked to the shore by a stone bridge that allowed the faithful to worship at its Benten Shrine.

In its entirety, Ueno Hill was designed as a collection of tangible references to classical cultural icons. The spot was particularly popular in the spring, when hundreds came to sit, drink sake, and perhaps even dance beneath the blossoming cherry trees.

Sannōsha Shrine

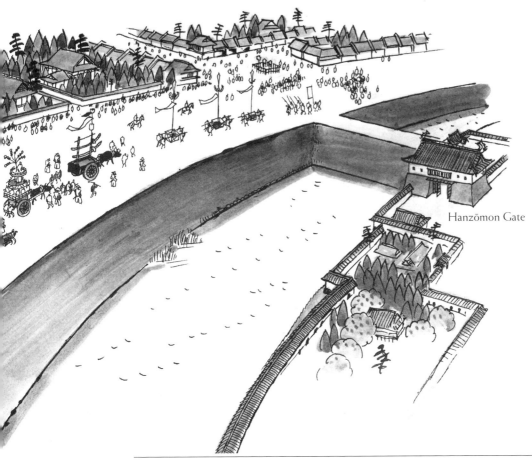

Hanzōmon Gate

The Great Festivals at Sannōsha and Kanda Myōjin Shrines

Another religion was growing along with Buddhism at the beginning of the Edo period: Christianity. That faith had been introduced in Kyushu nearly a century earlier, in 1549, by the Jesuit missionary St. Francis Xavier. It flourished during the regimes of Nobunaga and Hideyoshi, and Ieyasu too built a Christian church in 1599, at a location in Edo no longer known.

But in 1612 the shogunate proscribed the Christian religion and destroyed Ieyasu's church. Two years later the shogunate executed twenty-two adherents of the religion, and in 1637–38 it put down the Shimabara Uprising of Christians in Kyushu. To prevent further Christian expansion, the shogunate initiated the practice of "sect checking" (*shūmon aratame*), which required all citizens to officially identify the religious sect to which they belonged. The law was promulgated by the magistrates of temples and shrines, who had jurisdiction over the clerical institutions of the city, in contradistinction to the city magistrates, who oversaw the townspeople.

The most famous Shinto establishments under their purview in Edo were Sannōsha and Kanda Myōjin shrines. Sannōsha served the townspeople in the south and west of the city, and Kanda Myōjin, those in the north and east. The annual shrine festivals were officially recognized as "national festivals" (*tenka matsuri*), Sannōsha's being held on the fifteenth of the sixth month and Kanda Myōjin's on the fifteenth of the ninth, with larger observances held every other year. Vast sums were spent on these festivals, and some of the faithful are said to have gone into debt for the occasions. The shogunate tried time and again to curtail such extravagance, but to no avail.

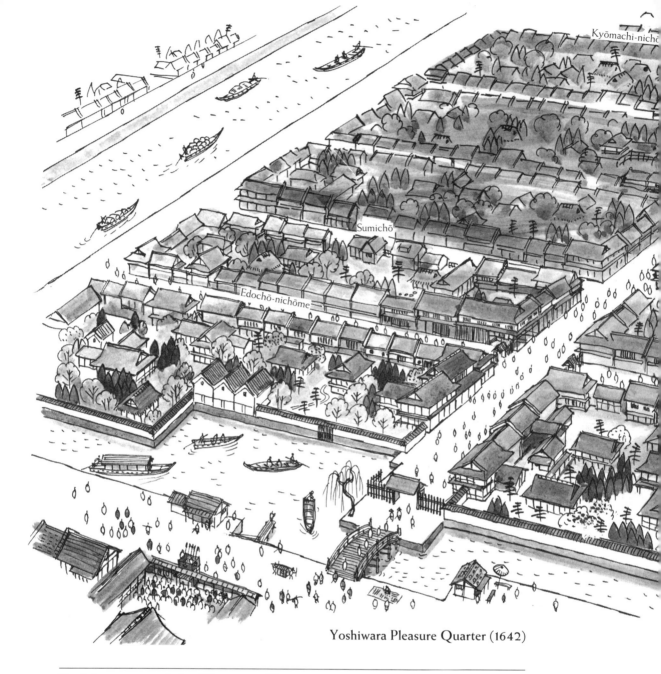

Kyōmachi-nichō

Sumichō

Edochō-nichōme

Yoshiwara Pleasure Quarter (1642)

Bathhouses and the Pleasure Quarter

For a full half-century after Ieyasu entered Edo, the city contained many rough, hard-working construction men but relatively few women. Whereas most cities had an equal number of both sexes, in Edo men outnumbered women by more than two to one. The city was still barren, dusty, and lacking in amenities. One of the few pleasures available to the working man was the public bath (*sentō*), the first of which was established by Ise Yoichi in 1591, soon after the city itself, near Zenigamebashi Bridge. By 1630 most city blocks boasted *sentō*, where men could enjoy not only a bath but, if they wished, also one of the bathhouse women, called *yuna*.

Even more prosperous than the public baths was the pleasure quarter (*yūkaku*). Already by 1610 there were twenty brothels at Dōsangashi and fifteen or so at Kamakuragashi and Kōjimachi Hatchōme. Some years later, Shōji Jin'emon asked

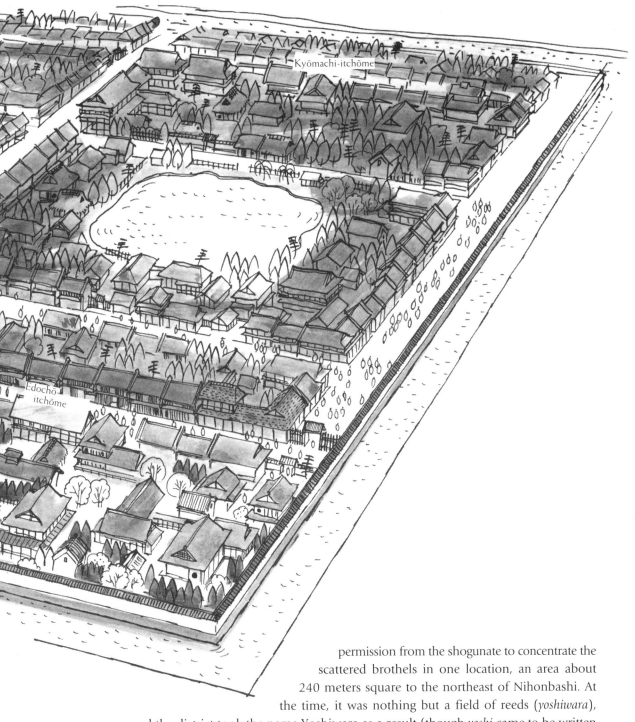

Kyōmachi-itchōme

Edochō-itchōme

permission from the shogunate to concentrate the scattered brothels in one location, an area about 240 meters square to the northeast of Nihonbashi. At the time, it was nothing but a field of reeds (*yoshiwara*), and the district took the name Yoshiwara as a result (though *yoshi* came to be written with a homophonous character meaning good fortune). In 1615 this licensed pleasure quarter was enclosed by a canal and entered by a single gate at the north. The interior was divided into five blocks: Edochō Itchōme, Edochō Nichōme, Kyōmachi Itchōme, Kyōmachi Nichōme, and Sumichō. By 1642 the pleasure quarter contained a remarkable 125 houses.

Yoshiwara was generally the preserve of daimyo and the warrior class. But monied townsmen gradually began appearing there as well. Yoshiwara had a more cultured atmosphere than that of the bathhouses, and one might sip tea there while watching the dancing of beautiful and talented courtesans.

The Kabuki Theater

Another diversion in the city that transcended class divisions was the kabuki theater. Kabuki is said to have been founded in Kyoto in 1603 by a Shinto priestess from Izumo Shrine named Okuni, who performed in male costume. The art was soon performed on the riverside of Kyoto's Kamogawa River, to great acclaim. It then came to Edo, where it took the city by storm, being patronized by warriors and townspeople alike.

Early kabuki combined simple theatricals with sexual allure, and the shogunate soon banned women's kabuki as injurious to public morality. All roles, regardless of gender, were thereafter performed by men, with those specializing in female roles being called *onnagata*. Gradually the focus shifted from eroticism to acting skill and to better scripts, partly under the influence of the puppet theater (*bunraku*), another popular dramatic form at the time. Eventually kabuki matured into a major art form, employing huge casts of actors, gorgeous costumes and sets, and orchestras to provide musical accompaniment.

A theater was built in the city in 1624 by Nakabashi Bridge, between Nihonbashi and Kyōbashi. It presented circus stunts and puppets, but its biggest attraction was the Nakamuraza troupe of Nakamura Kanzaburō, which presented kabuki plays that were the talk of the city. Though there were earlier theatricals presented in Edo, Kan-

zaburō's name is popularly associated with the real start of kabuki there. The theater was moved in 1632 to Negichō, north of Yoshiwara.

Two years later, a new theater was established in Sakaichō, on the west side of Yoshiwara, by a competing troupe, the Murayamaza (later called the Ichimuraza) of Murayama Matasaburō. Miyako Dennai's troupe, the Miyakoza, had a theater there as well, and later the Negichō theater moved to the same location, making the theater district the busiest place in the city.

A new troupe, the Yamamuraza, opened a theater in 1642 in Kobikichō, followed by the establishment of the Moritaza there in 1660. The Yamamuraza and Moritaza in Kobikichō and the Nakamuraza and Ichimuraza in Sakaichō became known as the "Four Edo Theaters" (*Edo yonza*) and were famous throughout the country.

The theaters were open morning till night, and people might devote an entire day to the theater, eating and talking for hours on end while enjoying the action on stage. As nighttime performances were forbidden, the troupes prepared for the morning show the night before. Farmers who had come into town to see kabuki would stay the night with relatives or in theater tea shops, which entailed added expense.

Gangs

The various laws promulgated during the early years of the Tokugawa Shogunate were systematized under the third shogun, Iemitsu, providing a foundation for the two centuries of relative peace that followed. The constant violence of the Age of the Country at War (1467–ca. 1573) faded from popular memory, and skill at arms, once essential for survival, became a much more abstract virtue.

Young men of the warrior class, in particular, no longer enjoyed a sense of direction and purpose. Some so-called "bannerman toughs" (*hatamoto yakko*) formed gangs and went out looking for trouble, as did the "town toughs" (*machi yakko*), who copied them.

It also become fashionable, first in Kyoto and then in Edo, to affect eccentric clothing or hairstyles. The most famous of such dandies, called *kabukimono* or *otokodate*, was Banzuiin Chōbei (d. 1650). But later cultural fashions ironically left those trend-setters behind, and they degenerated into feckless dropouts. But while their iconoclasm proved short-lived and ineffectual, they were for a while extremely popular.

The Great Meireki Fire

By 1644, the metropolis of Edo covered forty-four square kilometers. It dwarfed the next largest city, Kyoto, which at twenty-one square kilometers was less than half its size. In a matter of few decades, the ancient capital city, the cultural center of the country for centuries, had been superceded by the young and vibrant upstart to the east. That growth had been facilitated in part by the spiral plan, which in theory could continue expanding outward indefinitely, as could the city's peace and prosperity. Or so it was thought.

But soon there came signs of disquiet and disruption. In 1651, for example, the third Tokugawa shogun, Iemitsu, died in his prime, at forty-seven. Civil unrest was growing as well, as shown for example by the uprising in that same year of Yui Shōsetsu (1605–51) and numbers of unemployed samurai who had been disenfranchised by the Tokugawa government. Arsonists in Edo also began setting fires, waiting for particularly windy days to do the most damage.

Such blazes began breaking out more and more frequently after the turn of the new year in 1657. Fire bells rang almost without pause, bringing the townspeople uneasy days and sleepless nights. Then on the morning of the eighteenth of the first month, a dry northwest wind blew into the city, raising enormous clouds of dust. That afternoon, when the wind was at its height, a fire broke out at Honmyōji Temple in Hongō. The sky grew black in minutes as the wind-whipped flames enveloped Yushima and Kanda, spreading universal panic. All roads out of the area were choked with carts piled high with whatever their owners could save, and there was little hope for those who fell beneath their wheels.

Presently the Nihonbashi area was engulfed, and then Hatchōbori, Teppōzu, and Reiganjima and Tsukudajima islands. Then the flames leapt over Sumidagawa River and laid waste to all in its path as far as Ushijima Shrine in Fukagawa. The entire downtown area was reduced to ashes, and the entrances to Sensōji Temple and Reiganjima Island were heaped with burnt corpses. It was not until about two in the afternoon of the following day that the fire finally died down.

The Destruction of the Castle Keep

The dawn of the nineteenth brought a temporary end to the nightmare of flame. But the wind had not abated from the previous day, and again fire broke out, this time at Koishikawa. Fanned by the wind, the blaze again tore through the streets to the lower mansion of the Mito daimyo, where it destroyed its buildings, roofed with wooden shingles. From there, it raced to the Takebashimon, Ushigomemon, and Tayasumon Gates, then jumped the outer canal and reached the north compound of Edo Castle. There, the flames leapt from the residences of the shogun's closest retainers to the great keep itself and engulfed the five-story structure. With its coating of black lacquer, the keep was designed to be impervious to fire, but the intense heat created a firestorm that blew open the windows of the structure and sucked the flames inside. The disaster was complete when the powder magazine was breached by the fire and exploded.

Soaring pillars of flame then jumped to the main compound, second compound, and third compound, razing one magnificent edifice after another. Shogun Tokugawa Ietsuna himself narrowly escaped to the west compound, though many did not know until later that he had survived.

The tidal wave of flame next reached Daimyo Kōji, and soon the air was filled with thunder as the heavy, tile roofs came crashing to the ground. The screams of those crushed beneath made the scene a hell on earth.

That evening the conflagration spread to the townhouses of Kōjimachi Gochōme, then turned like a crazed dervish to the south, where it destroyed the daimyo mansions in Sakurada. The flames then jumped the outer canal and reduced to ashes everything from Sannōsha Shrine to Hibiya, Shiba, and part of Zōjōji Temple before reaching the shore, where they finally burned themselves out.

The city of Edo and its magnificent castle, built with the most up-to-date techniques by three shogun over half a century, was destroyed in a mere two days. The conflagration, popularly called the Furisode fire, left behind only blackened ruins and claimed victims that may have numbered more than 100,000, perhaps one resident in seven or eight.

"Fires and Fights Are the Flowers of Edo"

The great Meireki fire was the worst urban conflagration in Japanese history up to that time. Many of the survivors lost their homes and were reduced to covering themselves with rush mats to fend off the snow and freezing winter wind. Some resorted to black humor, easing their trials with poems like this:

> In Musashi Plain
> there is nary a dwelling
> fit to enter—
> people come forth from rushes
> and into rushes they return.

This was a parody of the old verse quoted earlier:

> At Musashi Plain
> the moon has no mountains
> to set behind—
> it comes forth from grasses
> and into grasses sinks from sight.

The shogunate had rested secure in its faith in a city planned for an earlier age, never dreaming that its mighty castle and extensive environs could be reduced to ashes in a matter of hours. And yet the government was not stunned into inaction. The very

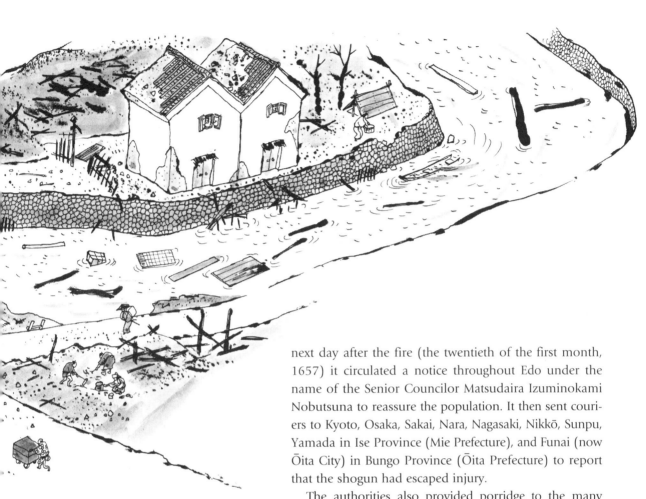

next day after the fire (the twentieth of the first month, 1657) it circulated a notice throughout Edo under the name of the Senior Councilor Matsudaira Izuminokami Nobutsuna to reassure the population. It then sent couriers to Kyoto, Osaka, Sakai, Nara, Nagasaki, Nikkō, Sunpu, Yamada in Ise Province (Mie Prefecture), and Funai (now Ōita City) in Bungo Province (Ōita Prefecture) to report that the shogun had escaped injury.

The authorities also provided porridge to the many homeless wandering the streets, expending a remarkable 900 tons of rice in relief efforts. The fire had reached the shogunal rice storehouses in Asakusa, leaving massive amounts of scorched rice that were also distributed to the hungry.

The system of alternate attendance for daimyo, set forth by military law, was also suspended, and financial support was provided to the daimyo, bannermen, and housemen. Even townspeople received 160,000 *ryō* (one ryō, or tael, contained about 15 grams of gold, with the buying power in 1984 of about 60,000 yen [perhaps 450 U.S. dollars]; see Seigel, xii, in "Further Reading"). These large-scale relief efforts were effective, and rebuilding began only a few weeks after the fire.

The great Meireki fire was not the last conflagration to destroy large parts of the city. But the city was each time rebuilt even better than before thanks to the resilience of the community, which shook off misfortune with the saying "Fires and fights are the flowers of Edo."

Taking the Measure of a Great City

The stunning effect of Edo's forty-four kilometer area in 1644 can be surmised in view of the fact that the average Japanese city at the time measured only two square kilometers. Even before the Meireki fire, then, Edo had outgrown the principles of city planning laid down for castle towns in the Azuchi-Momoyama period a half century before. Rebuilding the city after the fire therefore presented an entirely new set of problems to shogunal builders. A vital prerequisite was a comprehensive survey. The shogunate set this in motion only a few days after the last flames were extinguished.

The man put in charge of this work was Hōjō Awanokami Ujinaga (1609–70), an *ōmetsuke* (rather like a police magistrate, charged with daimyo surveillance) and an expert in the arts of war (*heigaku*). Under him was assembled a variety of talent: his adopted son Fukushima Denbei, the surveyor Kanazawa Seiemon, the master carpenter Suzuki Shuri, and Daidōji Yūzan, a specialist in Edo topography.

The art of surveying involved modern mathematical principles and was essential for producing charts. Until this point in Japanese history, maps had been drawn solely by eye, with features close to the viewer drawn larger. This empirical technique was completely unsuitable for taking the measure of an enormous urban center like Edo, and so trigonometric techniques introduced by the Dutch were employed. Even after the shogunate closed the country to most foreign contact, the Dutch were allowed a concession on Dejima, a small island connected to Nagasaki, which became Japan's "window on the West" and a source of new scientific knowledge. Trigonometry, for example, was brought to Japan by Caspar Schambergen, who spent seven years teaching it to his disciple Higuchi Gon'emon. The art was in turn acquired by the Edo surveyor Kanazawa Seiemon via his father, Gyōbuzaemon, and thanks to that knowledge he was soon involved in making maps of Edo based on scientific measurement.

These maps were constructed on a scale wherein five Kyoto *ken* (again, one such ken equalled 1.97 m.) corresponded to 0.3 centimeters on the map, a ratio of a little more than 3250:1. Not only was the downtown area reproduced on this scale but also the suburbs, to prepare for possible future expansion. Those outlying areas included Fukagawa, Honjo, Asakusa, Shibuya, Hongō, Koishikawa, Kobinata, Ushigome, Yotsuya, Akasaka, Azabu, and Shiba. When completed, this expansive map was guarded by the shogunate as a classified document. But public demand for such maps gradually grew until the government finally relented, stipulating only that the main part of Edo Castle be left blank. This opened the way for the publication of Ochikochi Dōin's "Great Map of Edo" (*Edo ōezu*) by Kyōjiya Kahei in 1670. Thereafter, a supplement, "Map of the Environs of Edo" (*Edo sotoezu*), was also provided, and in 1673 a complete set of five maps was made available to the public. These were the most accurate maps of Edo ever published, and they remained in use until the start of the Meiji period in the mid-19th century.

A Comparison of the Size of Japanese Cities in the Mid-17th Century
(the unit of measure is one square kilometer)

Major Cities

Edo 44.0 — 34.1 | 4.3 | 4.5 | 1.1

Kyoto 20.9 — 1.0 | 8.4 | 2.9 | 8.5

Osaka 15.1 — 3.4 | 8.7 | 1.2 | 1.8

Sendai 10.4 — 7.6 | 1.2 | 1.7

Nagoya 9.2 — 5.7 | 2.2 | 1.1 | 0.2

Kanazawa 7.5 — 4.9 | 1.6 | 0.8 | 0.2

Mid-sized City

Tsuyama 1.9 — 1.2 | 0.1 | 0.1 | 0.5

Warrior district

Townspeople's district

Temple district

Other

Yotsuyamon

Ichigayamon

WEST

Ushigomemon

Kōji-machi

Akasakamon

Banchō

Koishi-kawamon

Tayasu-mon

Torano-mon

Edo Castle

Kandabashimon

Shiba

Onaribashi-mon

Kanda

Shinbashi

Sukiyabashimon

Sujikai-bashi-mon

Gofukubashi-mon

Kyō-bashi

Naka-bashi

Nihon-bashi

Asakusa-bashimon

Tsukiji

Reigan-jima

EAST

Part of the 1670 "Great Map of Edo" (*Edo ōezu*),
made on the basis of precise measurements

Rebuilding Edo Castle

Thanks to the drawing of scientifically measured maps, the shogunate was able to begin rebuilding the city according to a plan designed to prevent another disaster like the Meireki fire. With regard to the inner bastion of Edo Castle, it was all too clear that a single canal had been insufficient to protect it from fire, and it was rebuilt with strategically located firebreaks (plots of land left empty to contain conflagrations). Also, since the wind in the Kantō Plain tends to blow from the northwest in the winter when fires were most likely, the upper mansions of the Owari, Kii, and Mito

branches of the Tokugawa house were moved from the main compound and out of the inner bastion. In recompense, the Owari and Kii houses were awarded larger tracts for their mansions in Kōjimachi, and likewise for Mito in Koishikawa. Parts of the vacated areas were eventually made over into a shogunal equestrian field and an herb garden. This redesign marked a fundamental shift from the policy in effect since the Azuchi-Momoyama period, wherein the shogun's close retainers lived in the inner bastion of the castle.

Reconstruction of the castle began on the fifteenth of the third month. The daimyo were again enlisted to support the project and ordered to rebuild the old stone walls ruined by fire. The palace structures in the main compound were magnificently restored in 1659, their roofs covered with fire-resistant copper or terra-cotta tile. The Ōhiroma (Great Hall; nicknamed the Thousand-Mat Hall) was simplified, and Shogun Tokugawa Ietsuna moved back to the main compound from the west compound, where he had been living for two years.

The foundation for the keep was rebuilt in the northwest corner of the main compound, where it had been before the fire. But just when construction was to begin on the five-story great keep, the shogun's uncle and advisor, Hoshina Masayuki (1611–72), pointed out that in view of the long-standing Tokugawa peace, building a castle keep simply for show represented an enormous and unnecessary expense, and in the end that famous symbol of Edo was not rebuilt, the city becoming a castle town without a castle keep.

Rebuilding the Warrior and Religious Districts

It was not only the mansions of the three branches of the Tokugawa house that were relocated after the Meireki fire, but also those of numerous other daimyo who lived especially near the castle. In particular, the tozama daimyo living in Daimyo Kōji were moved further away to make room for another firebreak. The daimyo mansions were rebuilt according to numerous architectural regulations, including a limit of three ken (5.9 m) on building width. Spacious towers and entryways were no longer allowed, and the magnificently colored carvings that had adorned warrior mansions since the Azuchi-Momoyama period disappeared from the city. The temple and shrine district too underwent a large-scale redesign. Old religious establishments near the castle were relocated. Sannōsha Shrine, for example, famous for its Sannōsha Festival, was moved from Miyakezaka Hill to Tameike. In addition, all the temples in the townspeople's districts, such as Kanda and Hatchōbori, were moved beyond the outer canal to newly developing suburbs. Nishi Honganji Temple in Nihonbashi was moved to Tsukiji, Higashi Honganji in Kanda went to Asakusa, and Reiganji Temple on Reiganjima Island went to Fukagawa. These suburbs became the new outer limits of the city.

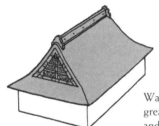

Warrior mansions before the great Meireki fire were large and magnificently appointed

After the fire, warrior mansions on the same sized lots were restricted in width.

The design of daimyo gates corresponded to the size of the daimyo's stipends.

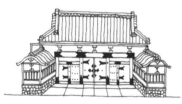

Daimyo of provinces

Daimyo with stipends of less than 50,000 koku (tozama daimyo)

Daimyo with stipends of more than 100,000 koku

Daimyo with stipends of less than 30,000 koku

Daimyo with stipends of more than 50,000 koku

Daimyo with stipends of between 10,000 and 50,000 koku

Rebuilding the Townspeople's Districts

To help prevent future devastating fires, the shogunate supplemented the firebreaks it built in the inner bastion of Edo Castle with other firebreaks and embankments throughout the city. The earliest of these firebreaks were built in Nakabashi, Nagasa-kichō, and Daikuchō; they were then followed by others throughout the city when the local residents could be relocated to make room for them. For example, when the Renjakuchō district by Sujikaibashimon Gate—an important junction for traffic to the Nakasendō Highroad beyond the outer canal—was designated a firebreak area to protect the important bridge there from possible fire, all the residents were moved to a suburb in Musashino Plain named Renjaku Shinden (Renjaku New Fields, now Mitaka City), where they brought new land under cultivation.

One new embankment was built by moving seven entire districts from Shirogane in Kanda to Yanagihara. It stood more than seven meters high and was topped with pine trees, noted for their resistance to fire. Another was built along Nihonbashigawa

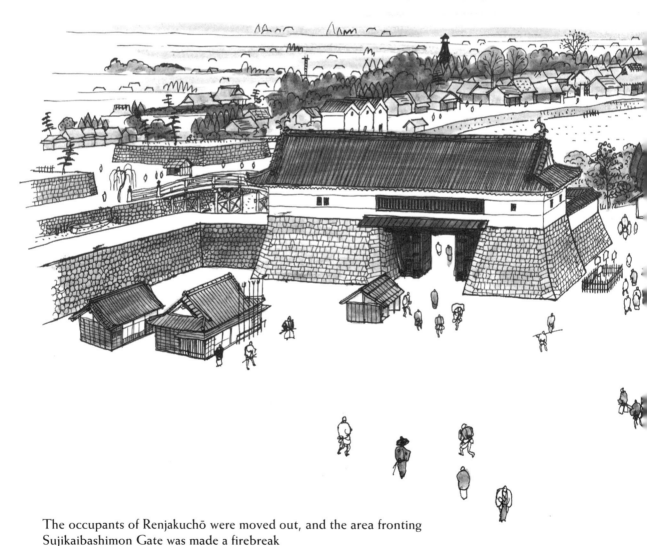

The occupants of Renjakuchō were moved out, and the area fronting Sujikaibashimon Gate was made a firebreak

River at Nihonbashi Yokkaichichō. Thanks to these new constructions, the most thriving centers of the city acquired pleasant greenways.

Together with the construction of firebreaks and embankments, roads through the townspeople's districts were also widened in reaction to the large numbers of deaths that had resulted when the narrow roads had become choked with fleeing residents. Tōrichōsuji Avenue in Nihonbashi measured more than eighteen meters across, and Honchōdōri Avenue, nearly fourteen. The smaller roads were doubled in size from about six to between about ten and twelve meters.

New regulations were also established for townhouse construction. Three-story construction was prohibited, and houses facing the street had to have verandas nearly two meters deep, so that in the event of fire, ladders could be stood on them to allow access to the roofs to fight the flames. Firefighting considerations thus considerably changed the face of the city, and the imposing three-story residences that had dotted the city disappeared until the late 19th century, after the Meiji Restoration.

Urban Growth

As a result of the rebuilding of the warrior, religious, and townspeople's districts, the borders of Edo expanded, once again demonstrating the utility of the city's spiral plan. The process was further accelerated as the shogunate assigned more and more outlying lands for the residences of bannermen and housemen, creating prosperous new suburbs.

Such expansion in turn necessitated an upgrade of the water system. The Aoyama water system was built to enhance the new warrior districts of Aoyama, Akasaka, and Azabu. Contributions by the Date warrior house allowed expansion of Koishikawabori Canal, which made it possible for boats to go from Edo Harbor all the way to Ushigome. This in turn led to the urbanization of the Koishikawa, Kobinata, and Ushigome farming districts.

The southern part of Edo grew apace, with parts of Tameike Pond, Kyōbashi, and Kobikichō being reclaimed. With the development of this new area, Tsukiji, the coast as far as Shinagawa became an unbroken cityscape.

Numerous temples and shrines were also moved to the area northeast of Asakusa, as was the Yoshiwara pleasure quarter, relocated from near Nihonbashi to a location close to Nihonzutsumi (Japan Levee) north of Sensōji Temple. There, it was expanded and renamed New Yoshiwara (Shin Yoshiwara), becoming even more crowded and prosperous as a result.

The eastern border of the city still ended at Sumidagawa River. During the Meireki fire, flames had reached the lumber, charcoal, and firewood stored in Zaimokuchō, Sumichō, and Takichō, helping spread the conflagration, and so lands on the opposite bank of Sumidagawa River, such as Honjo and Fukagawa, were newly designated as storage areas for those vital but highly flammable commodities.

Nishi Honganji Temple was moved to Tsukiji

A lumberyard was established across Sumidagawa River in Fukagawa

Nishi Honganji

Ryōgokubashi Bridge

Ryōgokubashi was the first bridge to span Sumidagawa River. When completed in 1660, it was simply called Ōhashi, "Great Bridge," but since it connected the provinces of Musashi (Tokyo Metropolitan Prefecture) and Shimōsa (Chiba Prefecture) it soon came to be called Ryōgokubashi, "Two Provinces Bridge," and the old name was forgotten.

A wooden span 175 meters long and more than seven meters wide, the bridge was easily the longest in all of Japan. It traced a majestic curve across the sky like a rainbow and inspired the people of Edo in their rebuilding efforts when all seemed lost after the Meireki destruction. Moreover, the bridge greatly facilitated traffic with neighboring provinces and helped change the city from a mere provincial capital into a truly national metropolis.

The bridge construction also spurred land-reclamation efforts in the area of Honjo, a floodplain. The method used was to divide the land into sections that were drained by newly dug canals and then filled in with the dried earth therefrom. The canal running vertically (*tate*) from the perspective of Edo Castle was called Tatekawa River, and the one intersecting it at a right angle was called Yokokawa ("Horizontal River"). An orderly system of roads was set out thereafter.

This reclamation project led to more construction in Honjo, including the lower mansions of samurai lords, and with it, the need for more drinking water. To solve this problem, the Kameari water system was begun to connect the area to a distant supply in Tamei, Saitama-gun.

The shogunate also built a temple, the Ekōin, at the other end of Ryōgokubashi Bridge, so that the prelate Jun'yo could pray for the dead of the Meireki disaster. It eventually become Honjo's most famous sightseeing spot.

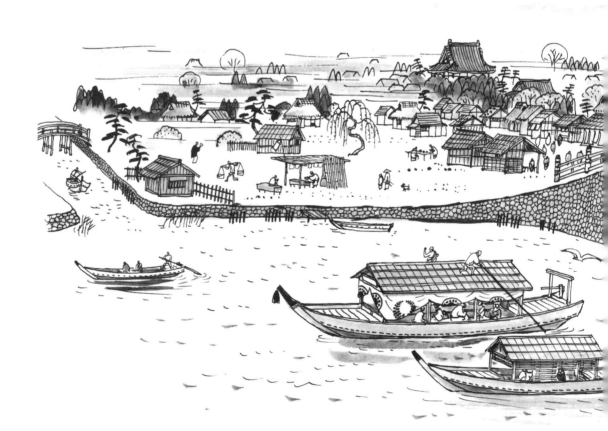

It was to Honjo that Lord Kira Yoshinaka—famous for his role in the story of the forty-seven rōnin or masterless samurai—moved his upper mansion from Gofukubashi. In 1703 he insulted Lord Asano Naganori, who then drew his sword and wounded Yoshinaka in Edo Castle. Naganori was sentenced to commit ritual disembowelment (*seppuku* or, vulgarly, *harakiri*) for the transgression, and his retainers later killed Yoshinaka in revenge and then committed seppuku themselves. This event became one of the most famous tales of loyalty and self-sacrifice in premodern Japanese history, and it is still a staple of the *jōruri* and kabuki theaters, with the title *The Treasury of Loyal Retainers* (*Chūshingura*).

South of Honjo was Fukagawa, at the mouth of the Sumidagawa River, an area known as Tatsumi ("Southeast") because of its direction from Edo Castle. Here were located the boatyards of the shogunate and the storehouses of the various daimyo, together with yards used by various lumber concerns. The devil-may-care raftsman who transported that lumber became another stock character on the Edo scene.

As the Fukagawa area continued to develop, additional bridges become necessary, and in 1693 Shin'ōhashi (New Great Bridge) was built, followed in 1698 by Eitaibashi Bridge. Thanks to these two new projects, local temples and shrines such as Reiganji, Fukagawa Hachimangū, and Sanjūsangendō began to attract larger and larger numbers of visitors, and like the commercial district in front of Sensōji temple, this area too became a lively entertainment center.

The 808 Districts of Great Edo

It was the Meireki fire that transformed "Edo" into "Great Edo," for the city grew from 44 square kilometers before the blaze to more than 63 in just a dozen years thereafter. Growth was interrupted in 1682, however, by another conflagration at the end of the year. That fire gave rise to another of the most famous romantic tragedies in Japanese history, related by Saikaku in his collection *Five Women Who Loved Love* (*Kōshoku gonin onna*, 1686). A greengrocer's daughter, Yaoya Oshichi, took shelter from the flames at an outlying temple, where she fell in love with a local young man. After the fire was put out she despaired of having another chance to see him, and so she started another fire hoping to be forced to flee to the same temple a second time. Half of Edo was destroyed in the two fires, and Oshichi was sentenced by the shogunate to death for arson.

But after each fire Edo rose phoenix-like from the ashes and grew larger than before. These "flowers of Edo" were calamities for the population, but they were also spurs to greater development.

The districts in the city had numbered about 300 in 1630, before the Meireki fire. To differentiate them from those that were subsequently developed, they were later

referred to as the "Old Districts" (*kochō*) and accorded special treatment by the shogunate. For example, when each new shogun was invested, the residents of the Old City were invited to Edo Castle where they were allowed to watch the nō drama, just like their warrior superiors. By 1712 the number of districts in the city had grown to 933, including 259 suburban districts (*machinami-chi*), which had originally been farmlands but were now accorded urban status. It seems likely, then, that by the turn of the 18th century, Edo first reached its fabled size of "808 districts" (*happyakuya-chō*).

The population of the city at that time was about 800,000, of which about 400,000 lived in the warrior districts, 50,000 in the religious districts, and 350,000 in the townspeople's districts. This contrasts with about 500,000 in London, Europe's largest city at the time. By 1700, then, Edo had become not only the most populous city in Japan, but very likely in the entire world.

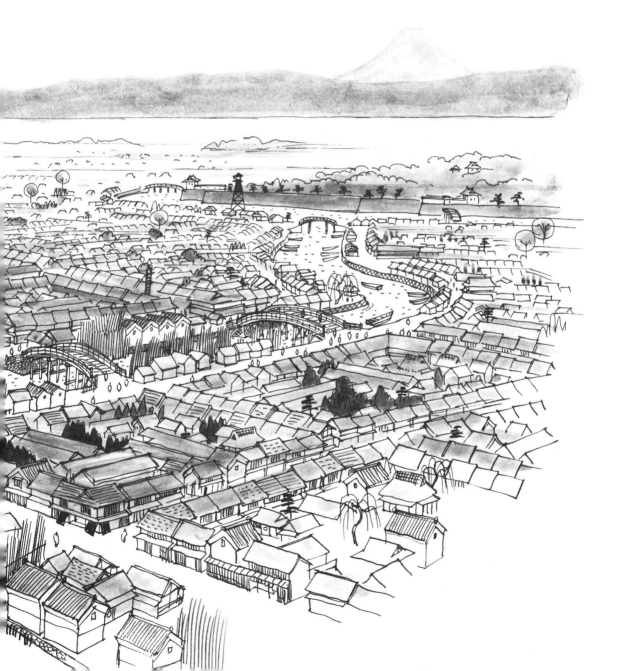

Echigoya Dry Goods Store

The Genroku Era

The Genroku era *per se* covered the years from 1688 to 1704. But the name Genroku is also variously applied to the time of the fifth shogun Tsunayoshi, who ruled from 1680 to 1790, as well as to the late 17th and early 18th centuries in general, when the culture of the townspeople first began to flourish. While often associated in the popular imagination with prosperity and extravagance, the Genroku era was also one of unprecedented innovation in urban fashion, entertainment, scholarship, literature, the arts and crafts, commerce, city management, and even firefighting.

By the time of the great cultural efflorescence of the Genroku era, Japan had been at peace for nearly a hundred years, and the veterans of the old battles of unification at the beginning of the century had passed away. For the new generation of warriors, the two swords, one long and one short, that had traditionally marked their class now remained little more than sheathed tokens of status, and fistfights and fires were as near as these men came to the battlefield experience.

But firefighting was a serious concern to the government, and after the Meireki

blaze it established four fire brigades (*jōbikeshi*, lit. regular firefighters)—one each in Ochanomizu, Iidamachi, Ichigaya Sanaizaka, and Kōjimachi Hanzōmongai—to be maintained by four bannermen with stipends of 4,000 koku or more, appointed by the government. About one hundred firemen (*gaen*) belonged to each of the four departments. The number of fire departments increased with each new conflagration, and by 1695 they numbered fifteen.

But these departments served only the warrior districts; there were none for the townspeople. There was on the average one major fire in Edo every six years, but each time the burned areas were rebuilt on an even larger scale. Such fires caused the price of necessities like lumber and rice to rise, and those purveyors profited, as did carpenters and plasterers.

But the warriors enjoyed no similar windfalls. Already heavily burdened by the system of alternate attendance, which required them to maintain huge establishments in Edo as well as in their home provinces, they were further encumbered by enormous rebuilding costs if their Edo mansions burned. The daimyo lords, whose incomes were tied to fixed rice stipends, gradually fell deeper and deeper into debt, while their ostensible inferiors, the townspeople, prospered.

Particularly successful were the great merchants from Ise, Ōmi, and Kyoto (now Mie, Shiga, and Kyoto Prefectures) who opened outlets in the new city. One of the most famous of these new magnates was Mitsui Takatoshi (1622–94). A native of Matsusaka in Ise, he made his fortune in banking and rice trading, and then in 1673 he opened a dry goods outlet, named Echigoya (pictured), in Honchō Itchōme in Edo. Ten years later he moved his main Edo store to Surugachō, and opened a moneychanging operation as well. He was named a purveyor of dry goods to the shogunate in 1687 and made an official moneychanger in 1691. By the decade of the 1730s, the Mitsui house was a truly national concern, maintaining seven stores in Kyoto, five in Edo, two in Osaka, and one in Matsusaka. These were the ancestors of today's Mitsui banks and Mitsukoshi department stores.

But the most famous of all Genroku merchants were Kinokuniya Bunzaemon and Naraya Mozaemon. Both profited enormously from their involvement in massive shogunal building projects after Edo fires and became the talk of Edo for their extravagance, spending more in the New Yoshiwara pleasure quarter than even the great daimyo lords. In addition, they denoted large parts of their fortunes to religious establishments. The haiku poet Kikaku (1661–1707), a disciple of Bashō, wrote the following verse about Edo's prosperity, noting that even slow-moving items like temple bells brought money in the city:

> Nary a day
> they don't sell a bell—
> springtime in Edo.

Ichikawa Danjūrō and the Growth of Edo Kabuki

The kabuki theater was a perennial favorite of Edo townspeople. As described earlier, there were four officially recognized theaters in Edo—Nakamuraza and Ichimuraza in Sakaichō and Yamamuraza and Moritaza in Kobikichō. But there was also a thriving kabuki culture in Osaka; in fact, much of the early impetus behind the maturation of kabuki and puppet theater originated not in Edo but in Osaka, in the plays of Chikamatsu Monzaemon (1653–1724). Counted among the three greatest writers of the Edo period along with Bashō and Saikaku, he is famous today particularly for his tragedies, like the puppet play *The Love Suicides at Sonezaki* (*Sonezaki shinjū*, 1703), in which a merchant and his courtesan lover kill themselves in despair over an insoluble conflict between love (*ninjō*) and social obligation (*giri*).

Whereas such western actors as Sakata Tōjūrō and Yoshizawa Ayame specialized in romantic plots (*wagoto*) involving young men and their courtesan paramours, Edo actors like Ichikawa Danjūrō (1660–1704) concentrated instead on action dramas (*aragoto*, "rough style") featuring hard-bitten warriors. Danjūrō made his debut at thirteen at Edo's Nakamuraza, appearing in the role of Sakata no Kintoki, one of the retainers of the legendary Heian-period general Minamoto no Yorimitsu who defeated the great "wine-drinking demon" of Ōeyama. Danjūrō painted his face in startling red and black for the role and struck menacing attitudes on stage, to great applause. His stage name Naritaya and costume crest of three concentric boxes (*mimasu*) soon became famous. Danjūrō's superheroes, who helped the weak and chastised evil, appealed to the rough-and-tumble tastes of the Edo public, who flocked to his performances. Thereafter such roles became characteristic of the Edo stage.

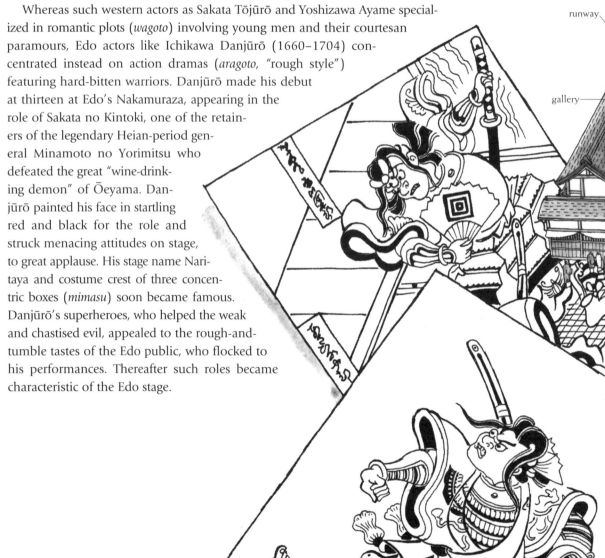

runway

gallery

greenroom

costume
storehouse

hairdressing
room

orchestra

stage

earthen floor

tower

public
entrance

The "rough style" roles of Ichikawa Danjūrō
were beloved of Edo theatergoers

The Poet Bashō

Of all Genroku artists, it is the haiku poet Matsuo Bashō who is the most famous today. He was born in Ueno in Iga Province (Mie Prefecture) to a samurai family in the Tsu Domain, and from an early age he showed great aptitude for literature. In 1672, at the age of twenty-eight, he went to Edo to seek his fortune as a poet and poetry teacher.

Upon reaching the great city he received support from Ozawa Bokushaku in Honfunechō, then went on to accumulate a large following, including Enomoto Kikaku and Hattori Ransetsu. Another disciple was Koiya Sanpū, a resident of Odarawarachō in Nihonbashi and a purveyor of fish to the shogunate, who provided a small house in Motomachi in Fukagawa for his teacher. The residence was anything but luxurious, for it was simply a rebuilt watchman's hut with a pen for holding fish until they were ready to be sold. A third disciple, Rika, donated a banana plant (*bashō*) for the garden, after which both the cottage and its poet resident took their names. It was here at this cottage that the poet wrote one of his most famous verses.

Sumidagawa River

Bashō setting out by boat up Sumidagawa River as far as Senju, where he disembarked and set out on his journey to the northland

An old pond.
A frog jumps in—
the sound of water.

But though Bashō now had a fixed residence, he continued to set out on one journey after another, in the manner of famous travelling poets of previous centuries,
like Saigyō. He departed on the longest of all in 1689, at forty-five years of age, with
the intent of touring the far northeast with his disciple Sora. He later immortalized
this trip in one of Japan's most beloved classics, *The Narrow Road to the Interior* (*Oku
no hosomichi*, published posthumously in 1703).

Having already let his cottage to others, he set out by boat up Sumidagawa River.
He was low in spirits, wondering if he would ever again see the cherry blossoms of
Ueno or the great peak of Mount Fuji in the distance. At Senju he disembarked, bade
farewell to his disciples, and set out for the northland, after composing this verse:

Departing spring—
birds cry,
and in the eyes of fish, tears.

Ryōgokubashi Bridge

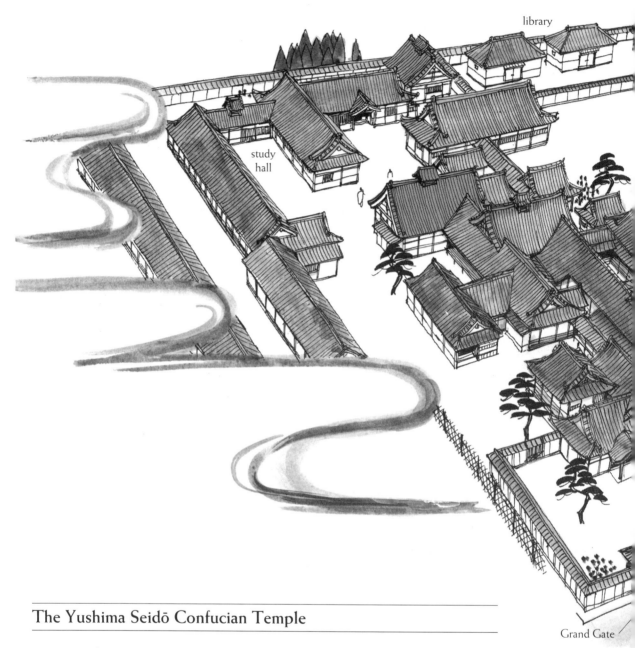

library

study
hall

Grand Gate

The Yushima Seidō Confucian Temple

In 1680 Tokugawa Tsunayoshi (1646–1709) became the fifth shogun. Seven years later he promulgated laws prohibiting the ill-treatment of animals, particularly dogs, earning himself the derogatory nickname of "Dog Shogun." Unable to produce an heir, Tsunayoshi solicited prayers from the great prelate Ryūkō (1649–1724) of the Shingon Buddhist temple Gojiin, who conveyed to the shogun a divine injunction against the killing of all living things, especially dogs, since the shogun was born in the year of the dog. The shogun thereupon established a registry of dogs, built and staffed enormous kennels in Ōkubo and Nakano, and commanded that anyone convicted of killing a dog be executed themselves. These misdirected laws were in place until Tsunayoshi's death twenty-four years later.

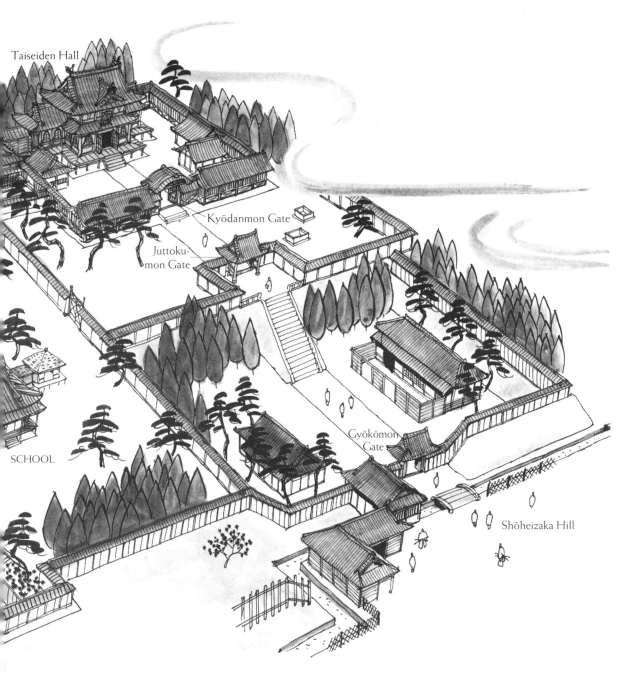

Taiseiden Hall

Kyōdanmon Gate

Juttoku-
mon Gate

SCHOOL

Gyōkōmon
Gate

Shōheizaka Hill

But though he was responsible for these excesses, Tsunayoshi was also noted for his cultural works. He built Gokokuji Temple in Ōtsuka and the magnificent Chisoku-in Temple near Kandabashi. And at Kan'eiji Temple he constructed Konponchūdō Hall, based on the eponymous building on Mount Hiei outside Kyoto. Tsunayoshi's Konponchūdō rivalled in size the Great Buddha Hall of Tōdaiji at Nara.

Of all his cultural pursuits, he was most devoted to scholarship. He moved to Kandadai Heights in Ochanomizu the Confucian temple that the great scholar and teacher Hayashi Razan (1583–1657) had originally built at his own home in Shino-bugaoka in Ueno (the location of today's Ueno Park). There, he had numerous structures added around a central hall, the Taiseiden, including a college of Confucian studies. The new temple was named Yushima Seidō.

NORTH

Asakusa Observatory (from 1789 to after mid-19th century)

Japan's First Observatory

Shogun Tokugawa Tsunayoshi established various centers of learning, among them the Poetry Institute (Kagakukata) for the famed literatus Kitamura Kigin (1624–1705, one of Bashō's teachers) and his son Kitamura Koshun, and the Shinto Institute (Shintōkata) for the theologian Kikkawa (or Yoshikawa) Koretaru (1616–94). In the field of painting he added a studio for the Tosa school of painters to supplement the preexisting studio for the Kanō (or Kano) school, the official painters for the shogunate.

But the accomplishment that had the greatest impact on subsequent generations was the first Japanese calendar, completed in 1685. The one previously in use was the Senmyō (in Chinese, Xuanming) calendar, invented in China during the Tang Dynasty (618–907) more than eight centuries earlier. The year on which it was based was slightly too long, and by 1684 a discrepancy of two days had developed, making it impossible to predict solar eclipses.

Yasui Santetsu (1639–1715), a *go* master to the shogun, set about studying new Chinese books on astronomy that had been based on newly imported European principles. Combining this research with actual astronomical observations, he became increasingly convinced that the old Senmyō calendar would have to be adjusted. The new one he proposed to the shogunate was named the Jōkyō calendar.

The shogunate rewarded Santetsu by appointing him to the Astronomical Institute (Tenmonkata), at which point he took a new name, Shibukawa Shunkai (or Harumi). At this time the shogunate put that institute in charge of calendrical calculations, instead of the Kōtokui family of yin-yang diviners in Kyoto, who had previously held that responsibility.

In order to further Japanese calendrical research, the shogunate in 1689 built Japan's first astronomical observatory, located in Honjo in Edo. Thanks to studies carried out there, Shunkai's Jōkyō calendar was further refined. The observatory was subsequently moved several times, to Surugadai Heights, Kanda Sakumachō, and Asakusa Katamachi.

The Kyōhō Reforms

While Tokugawa Tsunayoshi was responsible for numerous cultural works in Edo during the Genroku period, his handling of the shogunal exchequer was ineffective. Expenses mounted until the treasury was nearly bankrupt. The next two shogun appointed after his death—the sixth, Ienobu, and the seventh, Ietsugu—passed away in quick succession, but the eighth, Yoshimune (1684–1751), lord of Kii Province (Wakayama Prefecture), became famous as a wise and virtuous ruler.

Yoshimune made it his priority to reestablish the financial health of the shogunal government. He put an end to the luxury and ostentation of some Genroku-era warriors and advocated a return to the spartan philosophy of the first Tokugawa leader, Ieyasu. His motto was *kinken shōbu*, "live frugally and revere the way of the warrior," and to put these ideals into practice, he abolished nepotism and appointed men of ability regardless of status. The excesses of the past were soon curtailed and new policies were implemented, in a process later known as the Kyōhō Reforms, after the Kyōhō (or Kyōho) era (1716–36) in which it was effected. These were the first major reforms of the shogunate since its inception more than a century before.

It was the "south magistrate," Ōoka Echizennokami Tadasuke (1677–1751), who was most responsible for administering the reforms in the city of Edo. He had been the magistrate of Yamada in Ise but was then appointed south magistrate by Yoshimune in 1717, a position he held for a remarkable nineteen years, until 1736. He paid close attention to the needs of the citizenry and handed down wise judgments in legal suits, coming to be known familiarly but respectfully as "Master Ōoka" (Ōoka-sama) by the townspeople. The north magistrate, by contrast, never attained anything near the same respect.

One reason for the success of the Yoshimune-Tadasuke team was the suggestion box set up outside the law court at Tatsunokuchi, where townspeople could go and register opinions or complaints and have them brought to the attention of the administration. Thanks in part to this practice, the Kyōhō Reforms brought about significant results.

Magistrate Ōoka holding court

Koishikawa Infirmary and Sanatorium

Public Health

Most of the opinions submitted via the suggestion box had to do with ameliorating the poverty of the masses who had flocked to the city from all over Japan. To deal with the problem, the government first carried out a census of the national population. In 1721 Yoshimune promulgated an order requiring all the daimyo to report the area and population of their domains every six years. He also required each headman in Edo to compile a population register of the neighborhood under his jurisdiction, which resulted in accurate census figures thereafter. It soon became clear that the number of people living hand-to-mouth was much larger than had been thought, and plans were conceived to help them.

The first approach effected by the shogunate was to build a medicinal herb garden. Two such gardens had already been built in 1639 in the sub-urban areas of Ōtsuka and Azabu, where ginseng was cultivated primarily for shogunal use. But the Ōtsuka garden had been abandoned in 1681, and the one in Azabu had been moved in 1711 to the site of the Hakusan Palace (Tsunayoshi's lower mansion when he was still lord of the Tate-bayashi domain). In 1722 this garden was improved and enlarged. It was there that the scientist Aoki Kon'yō (1698–1769) experimented with grow-ing sweet potatoes to aid the population when the rice harvest was poor. This field is now the site of the botanical garden of Tokyo University. The Koishikawa Infirmary and Sanatorium were also established there.

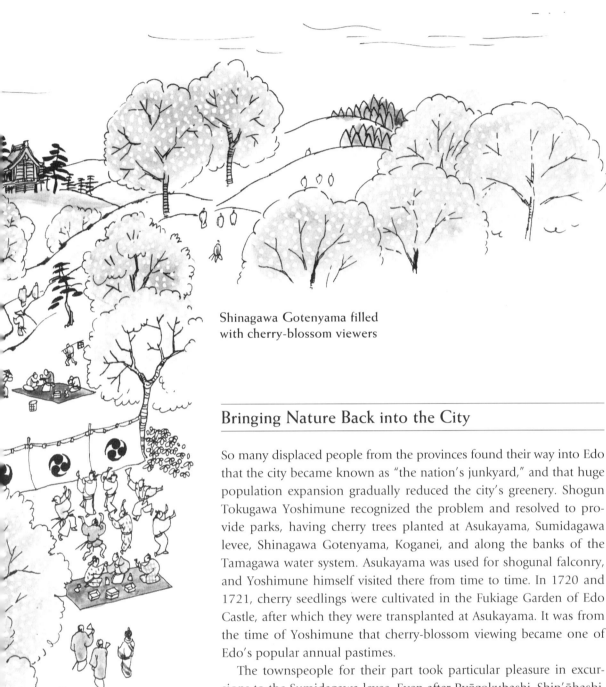

Shinagawa Gotenyama filled
with cherry-blossom viewers

Bringing Nature Back into the City

So many displaced people from the provinces found their way into Edo
that the city became known as "the nation's junkyard," and that huge
population expansion gradually reduced the city's greenery. Shogun
Tokugawa Yoshimune recognized the problem and resolved to provide parks, having cherry trees planted at Asukayama, Sumidagawa
levee, Shinagawa Gotenyama, Koganei, and along the banks of the
Tamagawa water system. Asukayama was used for shogunal falconry,
and Yoshimune himself visited there from time to time. In 1720 and
1721, cherry seedlings were cultivated in the Fukiage Garden of Edo
Castle, after which they were transplanted at Asukayama. It was from
the time of Yoshimune that cherry-blossom viewing became one of
Edo's popular annual pastimes.

The townspeople for their part took particular pleasure in excur-
sions to the Sumidagawa levee. Even after Ryōgokubashi, Shin'ōhashi,
and Eitaibashi bridges brought Sumidagawa River within the confines
of the city proper, Asakusa laver, Asakusa carp, and even whitefish could
still be taken from the river, and its crystalline water was used for
brewing sake. Townspeople flocked to its banks to enjoy the blossoms
in spring, the evening cool in summer, the moon in autumn, and the
snow in winter.

Nor was the move to bring nature back into the city limited to the
suburbs, for Yoshimune also directed that certain Edo Castle walls be
torn down and pines be planted in their place. The pleasing aesthetic
result can still be appreciated at the Imperial Palace today. These
measures made Edo a far more attractive living environment.

Fire Brigades

After the Meireki disaster, it will be recalled, fire-fighting measures were instituted in the warrior districts of the city, and eventually fire brigades were established under the direct control of the shogunate. This mirrored the earlier practice of daimyo maintaining fire brigades (*daimyōbikeshi*) in their home domains. One particularly famous example of the latter was the fire brigade of the Maeda lords, rulers of the rich Kaga domain, valued at one million *koku*. Its approximately one hundred stalwart firemen, called Kaga Steeplejacks (Kaga Tobi), became so famous that they later figured in the theater.

pump

When the cry "Fire!" was raised, such firemen dropped whatever they were doing and rushed to battle the blazing "flowers of Edo." But their tools were inadequate—they did have a pump, but its low pressure made it so ineffective that simple water buckets were usually preferred. Firefighters also used hooks and axes to tear down structures to contain the flames. When a wind sprang up, they would take up positions downwind and wave huge fans to beat back the flames, at the risk of their own lives.

Still, it was impossible to make Great Edo, which had grown by leaps and bounds to 1,600 districts, completely fireproof. In order to do everything possible to prevent future disasters, south magistrate Ōoka Tadasuke instituted town fire brigades (*machibikeshi*) to complement those of the shogunate and the daimyo lords. Thirty firefighters were allotted to each district, and eventually they were organized into forty-eight brigades, each of which was identified by one of the forty-eight syllables in the traditional *i-ro-ha* syllabary (except that *he*, *ra*, *hi*, and *n* had inappropriate linguistic associations and were replaced by "hundred," "thousand," "ten thousand," and "source," respectively). They were therefore known as the "i-ro-ha brigades." The brigade in the illustration is identifiable by the syllable *yo* (よ) that each fireman wears on his back.

In 1720 these town fire brigades were allowed to carry their own identifying standards (*matoi*), a privilege hitherto enjoyed only by the warrior brigades. Such standards had originally been used on the battlefield to indicate a general's position, and they were therefore appropriate for indicating the position of the firechief at a blaze. A popular song of the time spoke of the glamour associated with such *matoi*: "Shiba-born, Kanda-bred, and now standard-bearer of a fire brigade!"

The forty-eight town brigades were responsible for dealing with fires to the west of Sumidagawa River. Another sixteen were formed for the Honjo and Fukagawa areas to the east. All together, they included more than ten thousand men, and they made

watch ladder

standard

police station

firefighting tub
and buckets

Edo considerably safer from fire than before, though fierce competition between
brigades sometimes led to brawls.

Another useful innovation were watchtowers (*hinomi*), which in the case of shogunal brigades were more than nine meters tall. Tall structures were initially prohibited
in the townspeople's quarters, but smaller, removable towers were nevertheless allowed
atop the houses of local leaders, who were appointed annually. After the town fire-
brigade system was inaugurated, permanent watch ladders (*waku hinomi*) of nearly
three meters in height were built above particularly tall houses, one for every two
square *chō* (about 236.4 m²). Such watch ladders increased in height with each new
fire, to the point where structures eight meters tall came to be built atop local police
stations. Inside were kept the brigade standard, fire hooks, and buckets.

The tallest of all were the lookout towers (*hinomiyagura*), structures more than
twenty-one meters tall that were apportioned one per ten *chō*. The manner of striking
the firebell indicated how far away the flames were: single rings meant a distant
blaze, double rings indicated the danger of a major fire and alerted the local firefighters, and continuous rings meant a blaze nearby. The minute they heard the alarm, the
sons of Edo donned their headbands of twisted cloth and rushed out to battle the
flames.

Fireproof Architecture

Despite the establishment of fire brigades for both the military and townspeople, Edo could ever be completely protected from fire, given the city's wooden architecture and high congestion. But the shogunate did what it could to make the city's buildings less flammable.

One initial approach was to ban tile roofs. One reason concerned safety, for during the Meireki fire many people had been crushed to death beneath roof tiles as burning buildings collapsed. Another was the shogunal effort to curb spending by the daimyo, who lavished huge sums on tile roofs for their spawling mansions. They were therefore prohibited from using tile except for their storehouses. Instead, townspeople and warriors alike were encouraged to roof with miscanthus, straw, or shingles, then cover them with oyster shells, turf, or mud as a flame retardant. This approach proved largely ineffective.

storehouse-style buildings

plastered-style buildings

police statio

Then in 1674, Nishimura Hanbei of Ōmi (Shiga Prefecture) invented a new type of light, one-piece terra-cotta tile called *sangawara*, which gradually replaced the heavier *hongawara* tiling previously in use (see illustration). The shogun, Tokugawa Yoshimune, learned of the new tile via the suggestion box, and in 1720 he rescinded the proscription on tiles, eventually going so far as to eliminate taxes on them and even to lend money to encourage their purchase.

Building styles in Edo came to be divided into three types, according to their degree of flammability. The strongest was the storehouse style (*dozōzukuri*), built, like Edo Castle, with thick plaster over mud on the walls, shutters, and under the eaves, and roofed with the new sangawara tile. The next was the plastered style (*nuriyazukuri*), in which the second story of the facade was plastered as in the storehouse style but the rest of the exterior was of clapboard. The least protected was the flammable style (*yakiyazukuri*), which was entirely of plain clapboard with shingle roofs. In the event of one of Edo's blazes, they were, as their name implies, utterly defenseless.

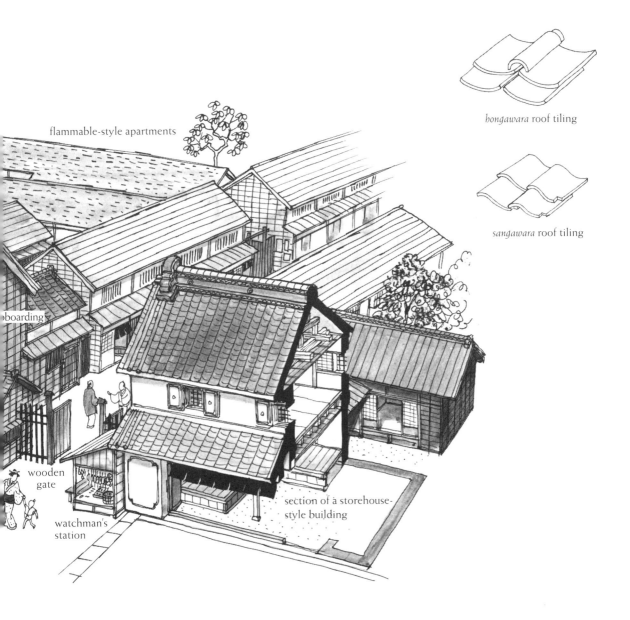

hongawara roof tiling

sangawara roof tiling

flammable-style apartments

boarding

wooden gate

watchman's station

section of a storehouse-style building

The Changing Face of the City

The proliferation of fireproof buildings changed the Edo cityscape. Already from the Genroku era (1688–1704) there had begun a gradual dissolution of the common practice of earlier castle towns whereby people engaged of the same occupation would live in the same district. Thereafter, the terms "commercial district" or "artisans district" remained in name only, and people of various occupations lived together. The succeeding half century also saw a great increase in the economic power of some townspeople, resulting in huge gaps in living standards.

The community of townspeople can be generally divided into three levels. The highest of the three were the landlords (*jinushi*), including community leaders and purveyors to the shogun; they owned property fronting on the main roads, and their residences, built in the thick-walled storehouse style, might measure anywhere from

ten to nearly eighteen meters wide. The middle class of townpeople were householders (*iemochi*), merchants and artisans who rented property on the main roads, where they built plastered-style houses from about four to eight meters wide. Lowest of the three were travelling salesmen, day laborers, and such, who lived in flammable back-street tenements.

The fact that the storehouse-style and plastered-style houses fronted on the main streets gave a more uniform appearance to the city. In 1723, builders of new houses were simply encouraged to keep their structures as low as possible. But in 1806 a law was passed specifically limiting houses to 7.3 meters in height. The walls of houses in the storehouse and plastered styles were covered with lime or oyster shell infused with India ink, which resulted in shiny black exteriors. The great stores took pride in their assiduously polished black walls, topped at both ends of the roofbeams with huge and sinister "demon tiles," which glowered down on the streets and were thought to ward off calamities and malign influences.

dustbin

well

latrine

Tenement Life

City blocks originally consisted of houses on all four sides, with the central common area left empty as a firebreak. But with the increasing use of fireproof architecture after the reforms of the Kyōhō era (1716–36), and with more and more people moving confidently into the city center, alleys were built through the previously empty commons and cheap, flammable structures erected. These were called "nine-*shaku* two-*ken* tenements" (*kushaku niken uranagaya*) from the fact that they measured nine *shaku* (about 2.7 m) wide by two *ken* (about 3.6 m) deep, for a total area of only three *tsubo* (about 9.9 m^2; one *tsubo*, about 3.3 m^2, being a traditional unit of architectural area). These tenements were not single units but were instead joined together, with several under one roof. Inside each unit was a kitchen and then a raised space in the rear, floored with four and a half tatami mats. Some had no storage space at all. The well (*ido*) and the latrine (*kōka*) were communal and usually located at the end of the alley, which measured just under a meter wide. There the wives would gather after their husbands had gone off to work, enjoying the now proverbial "meetings at the well" (*idobata kaigi*), that is, chatting while doing the laundry or drawing water for cooking.

The men who lived in these tenements were generally day laborers, palanquin bearers, teamsters, peddlers, and so forth. A few were masterless samurai (*rōnin*), but most were from provincial farming communities, and none had much money to spend. But they also paid no taxes, and when in difficulty they might apply to their landlords for help. Households averaged three or four members, a husband, wife, and one or two children—the beginning of today's "nuclear family."

The west bank of Sumidagawa River, site of the shogunal rice storehouses, was known as Kura-mae ("by the storehouses").

Moneychangers exploited their new-found economic power with lavish pastimes.

"Children of Edo"

By 1725, when the Kyōhō reforms were being instituted, Edo had become an immense metropolis of nearly seventy square kilometers. Though the townspeople were growing ever more prosperous, Edo remained above all a warrior city, centered as it was on the shogun's castle. While 12.5 percent of the city was composed of townspeople's districts, more than two thirds (66.4 percent) was occupied by warriors. But many warriors did not put down permanent roots, since the system of alternate attendance required daimyo and their entourages to spend much of their time in their provincial domains. Many merchants, too, were simply the Edo representatives of concerns based in the west, notably Kyoto or Osaka, and they were often sent to work in the city for a limited period, usually bachelors or without their families if married.

And yet by the end of the 17th century, the Genroku era, an image had developed of the quintessential Edoite, one who helped the disadvantaged and despised the toady, and who had spirit (*hari*) and chic (*iki*). The latter word, which came from *ikiiki*, "full of life," implied a focus on the new and the untried, together with sophistication, sensitivity, and eroticism. In the latter half of the century that followed, this image was combined with that of the *Edokko*, the "child of Edo," one born and bred in the city and proud of it. Typical of the latter were the fishmongers of Uogashi in Nihonbashi and the moneychangers who worked at Kuramae, by the shogunal rice storehouses. The moneychangers were early financiers, making their living exchanging cash for the rice with which shogunal bannermen were paid. In 1724, south magistrate Ōoka Tadasuke formally recognized the monopoly of 109 such moneychangers, which made their enterprise enormously profitable. Soon their extravagance surpassed that of the daimyo themselves, and they vied to outdo each other in chic and spirit, sometimes wasting ludicrous sums of money in the process. Those with a particular bent toward elegance and luxury came to be known as "men of taste" (*tsūjin*). In about 1770, eighteen such connoisseurs were identified as "great men of taste," and of these, Ōguchiya Yahei (with the sobriquet Gyōu) was particularly well known. He adopted the fashions of Sukeroku, a character in a play made famous by the actor Danjūrō II (1688–1757), then the rage throughout the city. Yahei paraded through the Yoshiwara pleasure quarter decked out in Sukeroku's purple headband and his paper umbrella with a bull's-eye design, showing off his particular sense of Edo chic and being boisterously greeted by teahouse ladies who called him the "god of wealth."

This developing culture of the Edokko came to be celebrated in kabuki plays, woodblock prints, popular paperbacks (*sharebon*), humorous poems, and the anecdotes of storytellers.

The Urban Metabolism: Water Systems and Sewers

The water system was one main source of civic pride, and all residents, warriors and townspeople alike, paid for the privilege of using it with fees called "water money" (*mizugin*), which were then used for maintenance and development. It may be recalled that the oldest water systems (*jōsui*) were those of Kanda and Akasaka Tameike, followed by the colossal Tamagawa water system project, begun in 1653. The Tamagawa system provided so much additional water that after the Meireki fire some was shunted off to supply other areas. In 1660, for example, underground wooden pipes were laid from Yotsuya Ōkido Sluice to develop the Aoyama water system (mentioned earlier under "Urban Growth") for Ōbanchō, Aoyama Ōdōri, Azabu, and Shiba Shin-bori to the south. Then in 1664, more water was directed from Shimokitazawa to Yoyogi, Mita, Meguro, Shirogane, and Ōsaki, then brought by wooden pipes from Tawarachō to Nihon-enoki, Isarago, Katazaka, Mitachō Matsumotochō, Shinbabadōbōchō, and Saiōji. This was named the Mita water system. And again in 1667 a project was begun to augment the relatively small supply from the Kanda system by bringing in water from Yoyogi. Three years later, yet more water was added by widening the Tamagawa system. In 1696, more water still was siphoned off from the Tamagawa system far west of the city at Hōyamura for another watercourse that was dug to Sugamomura and then extended by wooden pipe to Hongō, Yushima, Shitaya, and Asakusa. This was the Senkawa water system (in operation from 1696 to 1722), said to have been designed by Kawamura Zuiken, who is also remembered for developing coastal shipping routes. Because of these various projects, the Tamagawa system came to account for more than half the drinking water of the entire city.

Sekiguchi Dam in the Kanda water system

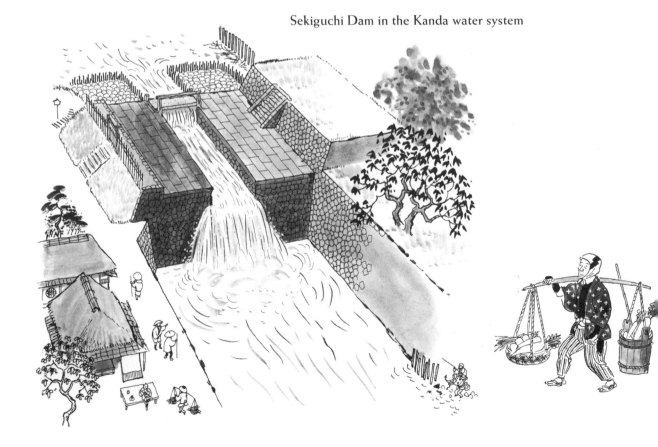

Such water systems were necessary because of the great difficulty of digging fresh-water wells in a city so near the ocean. One well generally cost 200 *ryō* to sink. But in the 18th century a new digging device called an *aori* was brought in from Osaka, which made it possible to sink a well of equivalent depth for only a little more than 3 *ryō*, which took much of the stress off the water systems thereafter. In 1722, the Confucian scholar Muro Kyūsō (1658–1734) advanced the hypothesis that the reason Edo suffered so many fires was that the ground had become too dry due to the large number of water systems being built. The shogunate, increasingly strapped for funds, used this eccentric notion to justify abandoning the Kameari, Aoyama, Mita, and Senkawa water systems, leaving just those of Kanda and Tamagawa.

Edo did not develop a correspondingly complex and wide-reaching sewer system, however. One reason was that scientific concepts of sanitation, such as those which motivated the development of the Paris sewers, had yet to evolve. But another cause was that human waste was a major source of fertilizer for the surrounding agricultural communities in the great Musashi Plain. Waste from downtown Edo was bought at high prices and transported to the neighboring farms, either by "fertilizer boats" (*koebune*) from the eastern parts of the city served by canals, or by horse or coolie from the districts further west. Such fertilizing allowed the cultivation of Sunagawa burdock, Takinogawa carrots, Komatsu rape, Senju leeks, Meguro bamboo shoots, and much other produce for Edo's million and more people. The garbage that the huge population produced went into dustbins in each district, and was then taken away and used for landfill at Eitaijima.

Edo water systems

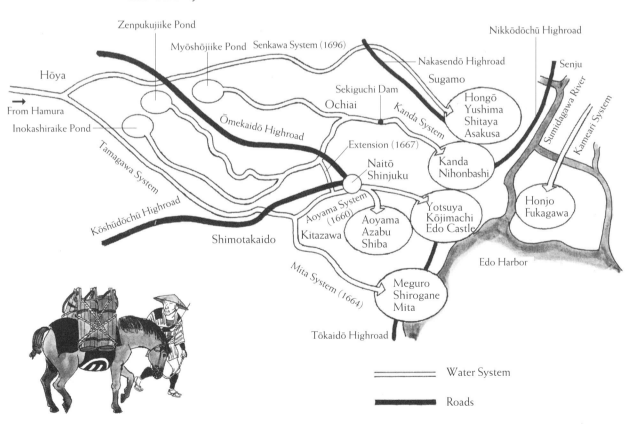

145

officials

The Kansei Rustication

In the spring of 1783, a drought upset the farmers' planting schedules, and that summer, rainstorms for days on end caused severe flooding throughout the provinces. In Edo a particularly heavy rain on the seventeenth of the sixth month left parts of Senju, Asakusa, and Koishikawa under water. The summer was also unseasonably cold, and day after day people wore their winter clothes.

Adding further to the misery was an eruption of Mount Asama in the seventh month, which covered an enormous portion of the northern Kantō area with ash and destroyed vast amounts of produce and livestock. In Edo it turned day to night, and soon Edogawa River began bringing down broken trees, debris from ruined houses, and parts of animal and human corpses.

It seemed no coincidence, therefore, when a lunar eclipse obscured the full moon of the eighth month, traditionally the most anticipated and admired full moon of the entire year. The event filled the population with dread, and sure enough, the climatic irregularities earlier in the year resulted in almost no harvest in the fall. The failure of the crops was a nationwide disaster, reportedly resulting in 200,000 deaths from starvation in the northeast alone.

For many farmers already suffering from high taxes, the great famine was, so to speak, the last straw, and they left their lands to find work as day laborers in Edo, inundating the city. Soon the city was overflowing with drifters and the homeless, and crime soared. Rice prices also skyrocketed, filling the poorer inhabitants with despair.

Eventually in 1787, rice riots broke out in Osaka and then spread across the country. Nearly a thousand buildings in the Kuramae storehouse district were broken into

Buddhist priest

Facilities for the homeless and dispossessed

during three days of looting, to say nothing of other storehouses across the city.

At this point in the crisis, Matsudaira Sadanobu (1758–1829) was appointed a senior councilor (*rōjū*) at only twenty-nine years of age. This precocious young councilor immediately began issuing laws to stabilize prices and keep the peace. These measures came to be known as the Kansei Reforms.

Sadanobu focused on the problems of the lower classes. In view of the riots of 1787, he had a workhouse built on Ishikawajima, where the homeless and the dispossessed of both sexes could be lodged. It was put under the administration of Hasegawa Heizō (1745–95), an official in charge of the investigation of fire and theft, who saw to it that they were employed and rehabilitated. But assignment to Ishikawajima was reviled by the poor, since the food and clothing there was inadequate and the labor was forced.

In 1790 and 1793 Sadanobu twice issued laws mandating that absconders be sent back to their farms. Popularly known as the "Kansei Rustication" (*Kansei no hito-gaeshi*), these laws stipulated that farmers be provided with travel money and farm implements and sent home. Other homeless were forgiven the crime of vagrancy and given jobs in agriculture or fishing. But the policy was not a great success, for it proved hard to keep people down on the farm after they had seen the big city; they usually preferred a life in the smallest urban tenement to the hardships of living off the land.

Academies and Temple Schools

Matsudaira Sadanobu also enacted educational policies to strengthen warrior spirit. In 1797 he formally turned Yushima Seidō into a shogunal college of Confucian learning. The hill on which the center was located, Shōheizaka, was named after Shōheigō (Changpingxiang in Chinese) in the land of Lu, where Confucius was born, and the college was accordingly named Shōheizaka Academy. The educational center for the sons of the warrior elite, it eventually became today's Tokyo University.

Originally it had been the norm for the children of warrior houses to be first taught at home and then sent to private academies and training halls for instruction in specialized subjects. But as emphasis on education increased, fief schools began to be established in various daimyo domains. One early example was the highly esteemed

Meirinkan in Hagi (Yamaguchi Prefecture). The role of such schools was to train the scions of the warrior class in cultural and martial arts (*bunbu ryōdō*), and they combined instruction in the Chinese classics with facilities for training with the sword and other weapons. Students generally enrolled at about six or seven years of age and graduated at between fourteen and nineteen.

For the education of the other classes, there were the so-called "temple schools" (*terakoya*). Such schools were originally places where monks taught local children. Toward the turn of the 19th century such sites proliferated throughout Edo. Already in the Kyōhō era (1716–36) about eight hundred schoolmasters (*shishō*) were teaching in such schools in the Edo area, most no bigger than two or three tenement rooms. The pupils, called "temple children" (*terako*), usually enrolled at about five or six years of age and attended school from about eight in the morning until two in the afternoon. In the morning they studied writing and received individual instruction, copying models of calligraphy made by the schoolmaster and being corrected by him. Afternoons were devoted to electives like reading, arithmetic, and etiquette. After four or five years of such instruction, students had mastered reading, writing, and the abacus and could graduate and go out into the working world.

Various teaching methods were developed by terakoya teachers. There were, for example, rigorous mid-term tests and final examinations, and students of thirteen and older were subjected to "cold study" from ten at night to two in the morning. In the summer there was class before daybreak. But there were also pleasant observations of the festivals of the Weaver Maid and of Sugawara Michizane, the god of learning.

One teacher particularly famous for his strictness was Kaminari Shishō, "Master Thunder," in Sanaichō in Nihonbashi. And yet that very rigor brought him numerous students from other districts. His school grew and grew, to the point where it reached nearly forty meters from front to back.

But running a temple school was no easy task, and schoolmasters did it mostly for the pride they took in educating the neighborhood boys and girls. These institutions provided much of the force behind the development of *Edokko* culture.

The Bunka and Bunsei Eras

The Bunka and Bunsei eras (1804–31) were the great age of Edokko culture, and the tastes and customs that matured during this period went on to form the bedrock of modern Japan after the Meiji Restoration of 1868. The Edo depicted in today's traditional comic storytelling (*rakugo*) and historical dramas on television are by and large set in the Bunka and Bunsei periods.

The most famous avenue of Edo during this time was Tōrichōsuji, which ran through Nihonbashi, and some of the most esteemed commercial concerns were located along it, such as Shirokiya Dry Goods (today's Tōkyū Department Store) and

Yamamotoyama (still operating under that name). In Surugachō in the north of Nihonbashi was Echigoya Dry Goods (today's Mitsukoshi Department Store), and further north, from Honchōdōri Avenue east to Ōdenmachō, were other dry goods and cotton wholesalers. Nearby in Tōrihatagochō was another great concern, Daimaru Dry Goods (today's Daimaru Department Store). And at Shitaya Hirokōji was Matsuzakaya Dry Goods (now Matsuzakaya Department Store) and a variety of other bustling large enterprises frequented by chic townsmen and townswomen.

Some of the most famous and popular districts in Edo surrounded this commercial center, such as Ryōgoku Avenue, the shopping and amusement area in front of Sensōji Temple, the New Yoshiwara pleasure quarter, and Uenonoyama, Asukayama, and Gotenyama hills—altogether too much to be enjoyed in just a day or two of sightseeing.

The Ryōgoku River Festival

The Edo year was punctuated by a variety of observances and festivals. Unlike today, the citizens of Edo used not only a solar calendar but a lunar one as well, in which the new year fell from about four to six weeks after January 1 by the solar calendar used today in Japan and the West. The first three months were spring, the second three summer, the third three autumn, and the last three, winter. The new year brought with it a variety of rituals held by warriors at Edo Castle. For the townspeople, on the other hand, it meant a much-needed day of rest.

   At the end of summer came the Ryōgoku River Festival (Ryōgoku no Kawabiraki), which gave the fashionable Edoite a chance to dress

up and go out to Ryōgoku Bridge. The festival, held on the twenty-eighth of the fifth month, marked the beginning of three months when crowds would throng Sumida-gawa River to enjoy its ooling breeze. During those three months Ryōgoku Avenue would be packed with passersby.

From about 1670, opening day was marked by fireworks provided by the Kagiya and Tamaya houses, one of which worked upriver and the other down. Warriors and townspeople alike sat either in pleasure boats on the river or in restaurants and teahouses on both banks to watch the display, and those who could not afford such seats crowded together on the bridge or on the shore, yelling "Tamaya!" or "Kagiya!" with each explosion above. It was a time for all to forget the trials of life and enjoy the willows, cherries, peonies, and white asters as they burst into blossom in the nighttime sky.

Sumo Wrestling and Sideshows

Spectacles like sumo wrestling were another attraction of Edo life. Sumo had begun centuries before as a court ritual, but by the 16th century it had come to be enjoyed outside the court as well; the warlord Oda Nobunaga, a particular enthusiast, liked to watch matches at his Azuchi Castle. Thereafter it became a popular practice for temples and shrines to sponsor fundraising sumo tournaments. By the 18th century it had become the norm to hold two major sumo championships of ten days apiece per year, one in the spring and one in the fall. Originally held at the Hachiman Shrine in Fukagawa, they were later moved to the Ekōin Temple at Ryōgoku, and the latter site was made the official one in 1833.

The golden age of Edo sumo was the era of the two grand champions (*yokozuna*) Tanikaze and Onogawa. From the autumn tournament of 1789 the best in the land were awarded the title *hinoshita kaisan* (lit., "universal patriarch") and a ceremonial rope (*yokozuna*) to wear around their waists to signify their exalted rank. The popularity of the sport climbed even further with the great wrestler Raiden.

Another favorite entertainment were sideshows (*misemono*). They were popular around Ryōgoku Hirokōji, near Kannondō Hall at Asakusa Temple, at Hachiman Shrine in Fukagawa, and in Ueno, where temporary structures for the events were erected and admission charged. There were generally three types of *misemono*. One involved stunts, including sleight of hand, magic, acrobatics, and martial art demonstrations. Another focused on the unusual and the bizarre, including freaks, rare plants, or exotic animals like elephants, camels, and tigers. And a third type consisted of handicrafts such as baskets, cut glass, mechanical dolls, and likenesses of famous people in pâpier-mâché, wood, or plaster. In addition there were miscellaneous attractions such as storytellers or peep shows. Female weight-lifters, equestrian stunts, and tightrope walking were perennial favorites. One especially well-known performer was Matsui Gensui, whose top-spinning act drew enormous crowds near Kannondō Hall.

Eventually theaters came to be built where all these arts—music, stunts, conjuring, dancing, and the rest—could be presented together. These theaters were called *yose*, and from the latter half of the 18th century comic storytelling (*rakugo*) was also frequently presented in them. By the decade of the 1820s there were 125 *yose* theaters in Edo, and unlike the kabuki theater, they were allowed to stay open at night. This popular art form continues to the present day.

New Directions in the Theater

The spectacle that above all others attracted visitors from the provinces was kabuki. After 1714, three great theaters remained in Edo, those of the Nakamura troupe in Sakaichō, the Ichimura troupe in Fukiyachō, and the Morita troupe in Kobikichō. The Yamamura Theater had been forced to close after Lady Ejima, in the service of the shogun Ietsugu's mother, clandestinely met there with her lover, the famous actor of romantic roles Ikushima Shingorō. Their relationship was discovered by the authorities and both were banished. The shogunate could not tolerate such mingling between members of the warrior estate and the lower classes, despite the fact that kabuki was immensely popular among warriors and townspeople alike.

But despite its continuing connection to the pleasure quarter and the concomitant shogunal disapproval, the kabuki theater was becoming by this time a grand art form

with its own venerable traditions. Before each actor could perform, he had to sign a one-year contract with the head of the troupe. The newly contracted actors were all showcased on the first of the eleventh month at an event called the *kaomise kyōgen* (lit., "face-showing play"). These debuts and the New Year's performances were major Edo events; they determined the fortunes of each troupe for that year and were the focus of special effort.

In the latter half of the 18th century, with the appearance of a number of superlative actors on the Edo kabuki stage, including Danjūrō VII, Onoe Kikugorō III, Iwai Hanshirō V, and Bandō Mitsugorō III, the theater prospered as never before. Danjūrō VII prescribed the top eighteen plays (*Kabuki jūhachiban*), including *Sukeroku* (illustrated here), and he became known as the "Thousand *Ryō* Actor," his income said to have been between one and two thousand *ryō*—a colossal sum for the time.

From the Bunka and Bunsei periods (1804–31) an increasing emphasis was placed on crowd-pleasing stunts. Perhaps the best-known play from the period was *Ghost Story of Yotsuya on the Tōkaidō* (*Tōkaidō Yotsuya Kaidan*, 1825) by Tsuruya Nanboku (1755–1829), with its grisly horror scenes. After another series of reforms in 1841–43 (the Tenpō Reforms), all theaters were moved to Saruwakachō in Asakusa, but the theater continued to develop nonetheless. One reason for this was the contributions of the non-acting contingent of the theaters, such as the prop builders, wig dressers, singers, and players of the *shamisen* (a three-stringed instrument usually played with a plectrum, first used in kabuki in 1633). The skills of the prop builder Hasegawa Kanbei were particularly important. He had been a carpenter involved in building

temples and shrines until the Meireki fire, after which he turned to making the enormous sets required for the kabuki stage. He and his successors (who each took the Hasegawa Kanbei name) demonstrated constant inventiveness in stage design. After a roof was constructed over the gallery, allowing plays to be presented regardless of the weather, they invented various new techniques such as the stage trap (*seri*) and the quick change (*gandōgaeshi*), wherein one backdrop would collapse backward ninety degrees to instantly reveal another. Another advance was the revolving stage (*mawaributai*), installed by the Nakamura Theater in 1793.

The twelfth-generation Hasegawa Kanbei became particularly famous for his invention of "tortoise-shell beaming" (*kikkōbari*). The shogunate had restricted the ceiling beams of theaters to 5.9 meters in length, which in the case of large theaters necessitated supporting posts in the middle of the gallery, which obstructed the view. Kanbei invented a way to assemble fourteen ceiling beams so as to eliminate the supporting posts. The design was first employed in 1856 in the Ichimura Theater, to great popular acclaim.

restaurant kitchen

Nihachi soba (noodles of wheat and buckwheat)

Kabayaki (fish fillet on a stick)

Tenpura (deep-fried fish and vegetables)

From Restaurant Teahouses to Noodle Stalls

Ever since the founding of the Tokugawa Shogunate, Edoites had tended toward a different style of cuisine than that prepared in the capital, preferring saltier and richer flavors to the more subtle ones of Kyoto. By about 1790 this style of cooking had become well established, and local seafood was served this way in restaurant teahouses (*ryōrijaya*) throughout the city. Two restaurants in particular, Yaozen in San'ya in Asakusa and Hirasei in Fukagawa, were famous for their *kaiseki* cuisine (adopted from the tea ceremony but suited to larger gatherings) and sea bream. Both restaurants obtained seasonal ingredients from the best sources and employed top chefs to prepare them, resulting in high-priced dishes beyond the reach of the average Edoite.

In contrast to these expensive establishments, a great number of cheaper restaurants and food stalls sprang up to cater to the huge numbers of warriors and merchants sent to Edo and living by themselves. They served general favorites like sushi, fish fillet on a stick (*kabayaki*), tenpura, or noodles. A particular Edo favorite was *nihachi* ("two-eight") *soba*, noodles made from flour in a mix of two parts wheat (*udon*) to eight parts buckwheat (*soba*). The name was doubly appropriate in that the price for a bowl was sixteen coppers, and the dish even figured in *rakugo* comic stories of the period. Noodle stalls were easy to dismantle and move anywhere in the city, to serve anyone at any time, even late at night. Edoites never lost their taste for that simple cooking, even though they might also take pride in spending large sums to enjoy the first bonito of the season.

Inarizushi (sushi rice wrapped in fried bean curd)

Tokoroten (agar jelly cut into thin strips and eaten with vinegar)

New Yoshiwara and "Hill Spots"

After the Meireki fire, it will be recalled, the Yoshiwara pleasure quarter was relocated to undeveloped land behind Sensōji Temple and renamed Shin (New) Yoshiwara, the earlier location coming to be known by contrast as Moto (Old) Yoshiwara. The new pleasure quarter was half again as big as the old, measuring three *chō* (slightly more than 350 m) east to west. It cost 15,000 *ryō* to move the quarter to its new location. Unlike its predecessor, New Yoshiwara was permitted to operate at night, and it also consolidated within its gates 200 previously disparate bathhouses.

Most visitors went to the nightless city by horse or palanquin via Dote Hattchō in Nihonzutsumi. The more self-conscious visitors might go incognito, wearing the wide-brimmed woven hats available near the gate. The central avenue of the district, Nakanochō Boulevard, ran north and south from the Great Gate at the north, with Edochō Itchōme, Ageyachō, and Kyōmachi Itchōme to the west and Fushimichō, Edo Nichōme, Sakaichō, Sumichō, and Kyōmachi Nichōme to the east. Both sides of the main street were packed with two-story houses of assignation (*ageya*) and broth-

Nakanochō and Edochō Itchōme, New Yoshiwara

els. The former were the houses to which one summoned the courtesans for entertainment; these were lavishly constructed, on a par with daimyo mansions. Only rich connoisseurs of pleasure could afford amusements such as these.

The pleasure quarter eventually developed its own distinctive culture that was idealized in ukiyo prints and in racy tales like Saikaku's *The Life of an Amorous Woman* (*Kōshoku ichidai onna*, 1686). Courtesans were given specific rankings, and the highest, the *tayū*, commanded great respect and equally great prices. There were male prostitutes as well.

But the fabulously expensive houses of assignation fell into decline from about 1760, giving way to simpler and cheaper "pickup teahouses" (*hikite jaya*) where one could obtain an introduction to a lady. There were also numerous brothels, "hill spots" (*oka basho*), uncertified by the authorities. At their peak, they are thought to have numbered about seventy in the city and outlying areas like Shinagawa, Senju, Itabashi, and Naitō Shinjuku. Fukagawa was the busiest of all, where one could find companionship far more informally than in Yoshiwara. Such places resisted official efforts to close them down, because their illicit nature appealed to the *Edokko* mentality.

Making woodblock prints

From Beauties and Actors to Cartoons

Brothels and kabuki theaters were considered necessary evils by the shogunate and subject to constant scrutiny. But Edoites were jealous of their pleasures and fascinated by the latest fashions in such dens of iniquity. One way those styles and fads were conveyed to the public was through pictures, not by the official painters to the shogunate, the Kanō School, with its focus on elegant birds and flowers or scenes of Chinese sages, but by townsmen-painters. Their paintings, called "pictures of the floating world" (*ukiyoe*), depicted popular figures and scenes. After the Meireki fire, Hishikawa Moronobu (1618–94) was a pioneer in producing such pictures in the monochrome print medium. Prints with simple coloration followed, and finally, in 1765, Suzuki Harunobu (1725–70) began making prints with a whole spectrum of colors, called "brocade prints" (*nishikie*). They were produced by taking the artist's original picture then carving a woodblock for each of the colors that would be sequentially impressed. Thanks to this process, color pictures could be mass-produced

Selling woodblock prints

cheaply. Particularly popular among the Edoites were the depictions of beautiful women (*bijinga*) of the Yoshiwara by Suzuki Harunobu and Kitagawa Utamaro. Such pin-ups brought a bit of spice and exoticism to everyday life.

Another favorite subject was actors in popular kabuki roles. One artist who gained particular fame for these was Tōshūsai Sharaku, who used sweeping line and bright color to represent the lavishly patterned robes such actors wore. As kabuki became more and more popular, demand grew for portraits of actors, particularly by Utagawa Toyokuni and his disciple Kunisada.

A third type of popular print was representations of famous places (*meishoe*). Two of the most famous series of this type were "Thirty-Six Views of Mount Fuji" (*Fugaku sanjūrokkei*, 1832) by Katsushika Hokusai and "Fifty-Three Stations of the Tōkaidō" (*Tōkaidō gojūsantsugi*, 1833) by Andō Hiroshige. Hokusai was also beloved for his cartoons (*manga*), alternately wonderful and weird, inspired by aspects of daily life of the late Edo era. The first collection of Hokusai *manga* appeared in 1814, and the final complete collection did not appear until after Hokusai's death and the end of the Edo period.

Dutch Studies

Pursuant to his Kyōhō Reforms, the eighth Tokugawa shogun, Yoshimune, encouraged practical studies as a way to improve productivity and welcomed new knowledge and technology from the West. The shogunate therefore authorized the importation of Western books, as long as they did not deal with the prohibited Christian religion, and set Aoki Kon'yō (whose experiments with sweet-potato cultivation were mentioned earlier) and Noro Genjō (1693–1761) to learning Dutch, as it was through the Dutch on Dejima in Nagasaki that foreign books entered the country. Foreign study was thus called *Rangaku*, from *Oranda*, Japanese for "Holland." The studies of the two scholars bore fruit, with Kon'yō publishing *A Brief Guide to the Dutch Language* (*Oranda moji ryakkō*, 1758), and Genjō, *Dutch Botany, Explained in Japanese* (*Oranda honzō wage*, 1750). After studying the latter book, Tamura Ransui (1718–76) and Hiraga Gennai (1728–79) resolved to cultivate Korean ginseng for its curative properties; then, starting in 1757, they held periodic exhibitions in Edo of new herbal remedies. Gennai also became the talk of Edo for his experiments with electricity.

The new interest in experimentation led to investigation into the workings of the human body, and in 1771, at the execution grounds of Kozukappara in Edo, Sugita Genpaku (1733–1817) and Maeno Ryōtaku (1723–1803) began the scientific dissection of corpses. Three years later Genpaku and his colleagues published a translation of *Tafel Anatomia* under the title *A New Book on Anatomy* (*Kaitai shinsho*, 1774). Toward the end of his life, Genpaku wrote *Beginning Dutch Studies* (*Rangaku kotohajime*, 1815), in which he recounted the early struggles by Japanese to learn the Dutch language and assimilate Western science.

Dutch studies also influenced the art world, bringing about more precise and scientific observation of flora and fauna and also the introduction of what were for the

An electrical experiment by Hiraga Gennai

Japanese exotic techniques of perspective. Ukiyoe artists adopted such perspectival techniques in their own works, with Okumura Masanobu (1686–1764), for example, using them to give his subjects a new sense of mass. His pictures seemed to float on the page and were called "floating pictures" (*ukie*) as a result. The same technique was used in the "peep show" pictures in the entertainment districts.

Shiba Kōkan (1738/47–1818) also experimented with copperplate prints in 1780, followed by avid practice with oil painting, another newly imported technique. Also interested in astronomy and geology, he introduced to Japan the Copernican model of the solar system.

Sugita Genpaku and Maeno Ryōtaku taking notes at a dissection

A painting of the Ochanomizu landscape by Shiba Kōkan, demonstrating a greater sense of depth through the use of new techniques of perspective

Popular Deities

Despite the allure of new Western science, Edoites continued to believe in the ancient Buddhas and gods and to pray to them for miracles. It was still the practice, for example, to worship at Chanoki Inari Shrine to cure eye ailments and at Takao Inari Shrine for headaches.

Some deities were thought to lodge in the humblest locations. Another place to go to cure a headache, for example, was Kyōbashi Bridge, where a prayer at the railing might prove successful. A prayer at the railing of Nihonbashi Bridge, by contrast, was thought to be efficacious for whooping cough. And one had to touch the iron in a wooden gate to cure beriberi. One rumored cure was enough to set the town abuzz, but if no miracle was forthcoming, the god was promptly forgotten. Such deities were therefore called "popular gods" (*hayarigami*). They could be appealed to not only for health but also for success in money matters or in conceiving and rearing children.

One example was the God of the Poor (Binbōgami). Lodged in a small sanctuary on the grounds of Koishikawa Tenjin Shrine, this god drew constant supplicants, who had started visiting upon hearing of a destitute bannerman who, as he worshipped a picture of the god at his home and made daily offerings of ritual sake, gradually grew rich. Even so insubstantial a "miracle" had considerable appeal.

It became popular to make pilgrimages to the sites of such popular gods. For those without the time and money for such activities, there was the Sazaedō ("Turbo Hall," a turbo being a spiral shell), at Rakanji Temple in Honjo. Inside was a spiral staircase

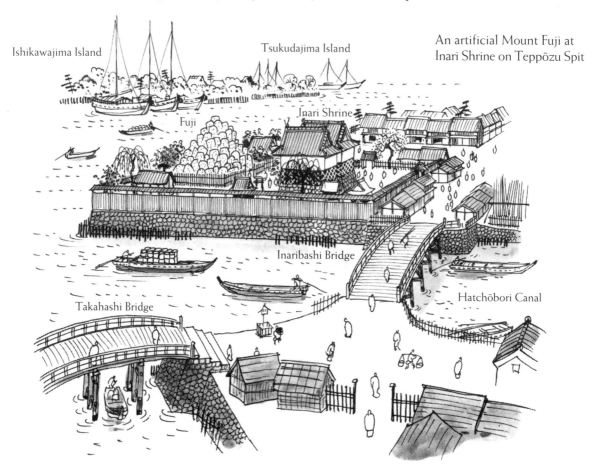

Ishikawajima Island

Tsukudajima Island

An artificial Mount Fuji at Inari Shrine on Teppōzu Spit

Fuji

Inari Shrine

Inaribashi Bridge

Hatchōbori Canal

Takahashi Bridge

which worshippers could climb to the third floor, praying to one hundred Kannon Bodhisattvas modelled after those in Kansai, to the west, and other distant spots. The view of Edo from the top was splendid, and the place became a magnet for tourists and worshippers.

Also popular was mountain worship, including the climbing of Mount Fuji. The mountain, the highest in Japan and visible from many parts of Edo, was taken to symbolize the Buddhist paradise of the Pure Land, and many of the faithful saved their coppers so that they could join groups and attempt the peak. For those without the necessary funds, there were various temples and shrines within the city where small artificial Fuji "mountains" were constructed as substitutes.

Sazaedō Hall in Rakanji Temple

Meguro Fudōdō Temple

Baths and Barbers of the Floating World

The Edo day started in the morning with the calls of peddlars hawking their wares. The local baths opened at about 6 A.M., and they soon filled with youngsters washing up before breakfast and retirees enjoying a leisurely morning dip. They were a cheap pleasure, at only six coppers for an adult and four for a child, and they stayed open till about six in the evening.

Edo had a paucity of wells, which meant that even many rich households did not have their own hot baths. Public bathhouses became favorite places for relaxation and a bit of gossip. Their atmosphere was captured particularly poignantly by Shikitei

Sanba (1776–1822) in *Bathhouse of the Floating World* (*Ukiyoburo*, 1809–13), a collection of humorous vignettes set in an Edo bathhouse.

It was not rare for men and women to bathe together, but according to the locality, men and women might alternate bath days, or they might use separate facilities. That became the norm after 1791, when mixed bathing was prohibited by the shogunate. Men's facilities might also have a room upstairs where the customers could relax after their baths and have a cup of tea and perhaps a game of *go* or *shōgi*. In 1810, ten bathhouse unions were established in the capital, and they counted 523 separate member houses.

Barbershops were another necessity for Edoites, and there were six locations where those in need could go: Nihonbashi, Tokiwabashi, Asakusa Mitsuke, Sujikai Mitsuke, Takanawa Kurumachō, and Kōjimachi. The shops stood next to the government's official notice boards, which the barbers were responsible for maintaining. They functioned much as today's beauty parlors and barbershops, and there were different hairstyles according to one's sex, occupation, and position in society, as well as current fashions for the barber to keep in mind. In the illustration, one man is having the crown of his head shaved in the traditional *chonmage* manner. Later the long hair in the back will be oiled and tied into a short queue (*motodori*) to be folded over the crown, in the fashion of the other men illustrated. A variant of this style is still worn by sumo wrestlers today. The barbershops were overseen by a union, though not all barbers belonged. These shops enjoyed considerable popularity, and the humorist Shikitei Sanba consequently devoted a volume to them as well, *The Barbershop of the Floating World* (*Ukiyodoko*, 1813–14).

Great Edo Traffic Jams

When Edo was rebuilt following the Meireki fire, the highways and byways once criticized for their great size were soon altogether too small to handle the burgeoning traffic. To stem the tide, the shogunate first prohibited palanquins to able-bodied townsmen below the age of fifty, save physicians and monks. Then in 1674 stringent laws were promulgated that stipulated punishments not only for the illegal rider but also for the owner of the palanquin and its bearers. But as some townspeople came to rival and then surpass the warriors in wealth, it became impossible to maintain such class discrimination, and in 1681 modest palanquins were allowed to all. In 1700 300 rental palanquins were licensed, and in 1726 that cap on their numbers was lifted. They were the ancestors of today's taxis.

Another ubiquitous vehicle was the two-wheeled hand-drawn cart for hauling loads. In Edo's early years, four-wheeled carts drawn by oxen were also used, but they were hard to maneuver and gradually disappeared. But the biggest hindrance to the smooth flow of traffic was the horse-drawn cart. The shogunate tried to improve matters by prohibiting teamsters from parking on the streets or leaving carts unattended. Beginning in 1716, causing a fatal traffic accident with a cart or horse could be punished by exile or even worse. Modern Tokyo's traffic problems clearly have a long history.

Demarcating the City

Though Edo continued to expand throughout the Tokugawa age, it came to be loosely characterized in size as "four square leagues" (*shiri shihō*). But even the shogunate had never precisely defined the boundaries of the city, and as seen by expressions like "Edo stops at Kaneyasu" (a notions store in Hongō Sanchōme), people had a very vague idea of where it began and ended.

After the turn of the 18th century, crime and other urban problems grew in number and complexity, and in order to deal with them it became necessary to define city subsections more precisely. In 1818 the shogunal judicial council (*hyōjōsho*) accordingly demarcated four specific urban subsections:

East End: Sunamura, Kameido, Kigegawa, Sudamura
South End: Kamiōsakimura, Minami Shinagawajuku
West End: Yoyogimura, Tsunohazumura, Totsukamura, Kamiochiaimura
North End: Senju, Ogumura, Takinogawa, Itabashi

These subsections corresponded to the modern area covered by Chiyoda, Chūō, Minato, Shinjuku, Bunkyō, Taitō, Sumida, Kōtō, Shibuya, Toshima, and Arakawa wards, together with parts of Shinagawa, Meguro, Kita, and Itabashi wards.

A chronological analysis of Edo maps allows us to understand the subsections of Edo in more detail. By the end of the Edo period, the entire area covered by the city had reached 79.8 square kilometers, forty times the size of the average castle town, which had not appreciably grown after the middle of the 17th century. The maps also show that while the religious districts did not change much throughout the Edo period, the districts for the warriors and townspeople steadily increased in size, with those of the latter group steadily outpacing those of the former in their growth rate.

The 808 districts of the Genroku era had more than doubled to 1,678 by 1745, then reached 1,719 districts by 1843. These figures underscore the city's unquenchable vitality.

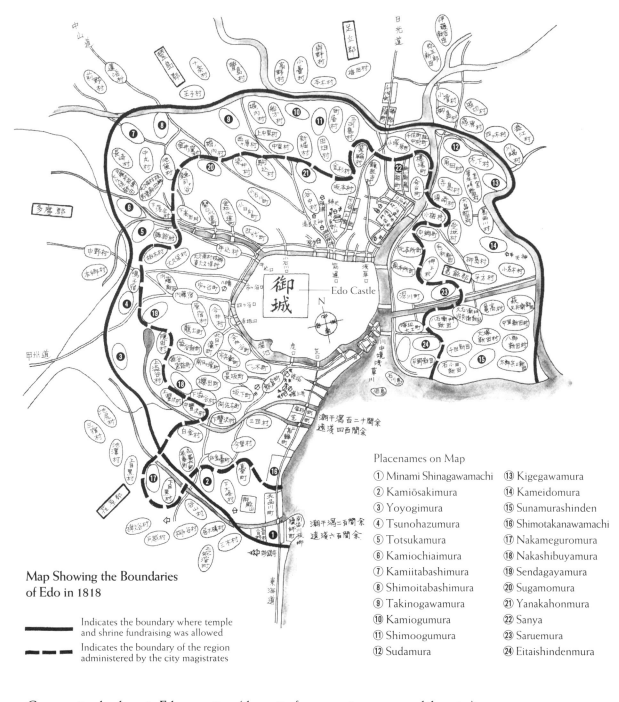

Map Showing the Boundaries of Edo in 1818

━━━ Indicates the boundary where temple and shrine fundraising was allowed

■ ■ ■ Indicates the boundary of the region administered by the city magistrates

Placenames on Map

① Minami Shinagawamachi
② Kamiōsakimura
③ Yoyogimura
④ Tsunohazumura
⑤ Totsukamura
⑥ Kamiochiaimura
⑦ Kamiitabashimura
⑧ Shimoitabashimura
⑨ Takinogawamura
⑩ Kamiogumura
⑪ Shimoogumura
⑫ Sudamura
⑬ Kigegawamura
⑭ Kameidomura
⑮ Sunamurashinden
⑯ Shimotakanawamachi
⑰ Nakameguromura
⑱ Nakashibuyamura
⑲ Sendagayamura
⑳ Sugamomura
㉑ Yanakahonmura
㉒ Sanya
㉓ Saruemura
㉔ Eitaishindenmura

Comparative land use in Edo over time (the unit of measure is one square kilometer)

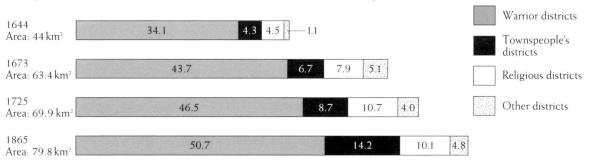

Warrior districts	Townspeople's districts	Religious districts	Other districts

1644
Area: 44 km² — 34.1 | 4.3 | 4.5 | 1.1

1673
Area: 63.4 km² — 43.7 | 6.7 | 7.9 | 5.1

1725
Area: 69.9 km² — 46.5 | 8.7 | 10.7 | 4.0

1865
Area: 79.8 km² — 50.7 | 14.2 | 10.1 | 4.8

Itabashi

Senju

The Four Waystations of Edo

In order to travel outside the four square leagues of Edo proper, one had to pass through one of "The Four Waystations of Edo" (Edo Yonjuku): Shinagawa, Naitō Shinjuku, Itabashi, and Senju. Each of these bustling waystations was about eight kilometers from Nihonbashi. The busiest of all was Shinagawa, the first waystation on the Tōkaidō Highroad to Kyoto and Osaka. By 1849 Shinagawa contained one *honjin* inn and two *wakihonjin* subsidiary inns for lodging daimyo and other important travellers, plus 93 other inns that stretched along the seacoast. There are said to have been 1,561 families living there, with a total population of 6,890, meaning that Shinagawa alone had by that time reached the size of a provincial castle town.

Naitō Shinjuku, the first waystation on the Kōshūdōchū Highroad, was established in 1698 where that highroad and Ōmekaidō Highroad diverged. It was the site of the lower mansion of the Naitō family, lords of the Takatō domain in Shinshū

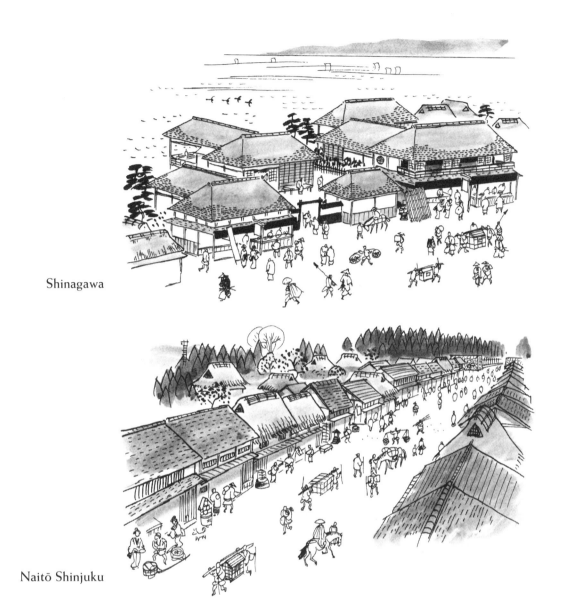

Shinagawa

Naitō Shinjuku

Province (Nagano Prefecture), and of the four stations it was newest, hence *shinjuku* ("new station"). It temporarily lost its waystation status in 1718 but regained it in 1772, eventually becoming a focal point of the western part of the city and the second most prosperous waystation after Shinagawa.

The other two waystations—Itabashi (the first station on the Nakasendō Highroad) and Senju (the first station on the Nikkōdōchū Highroad)—were hardly backwaters, for both served the enormous entourages of daimyo in alternate attendance to and from the Tōsandō, Hokurikudō, and Ōshūdōsuji regions to the north, northeast, and northwest of the city. Senju was actually divided into two waystations, the northern and the southern, and it also served as the point of origin for boats plying Sumidagawa River bound to and from Honjo and Fukagawa.

The inns in all four waystations were permitted to keep prostitutes, called *meshi-morionna* (lit. rice-serving women), whom the shogunate ranked a grade lower than the women of New Yoshiwara. In view of such entertainments, these four waystations were visited by many Edoites who had other things on their minds than distant travel.

Urban Congestion

By the beginning of the 19th century, the population of Great Edo had reached nearly 1,400,000. From 500,000 to 700,000 lived in warrior districts, 50,000 to 60,000 in religious districts, and 550,000 to 650,000 in townspeople's districts. Directives for the first actual census were not announced until 1721, but it appears that by that time the population was already about 1,300,000. By comparison, Europe's largest city, London, had a population of about 850,000 in 1801. Edo's population in 1725 broke down into 650,000 in warrior districts, 50,000 in religious districts, and 600,000 in townspeople's districts.

The population density figures are given in the accompanying table. Compared to the numbers provided in the 1980 census, the density of the Edo warrior districts, which covered about 66.4 percent of the city, was about that of Minato Ward in 1980, an area now composed largely of office buildings. The density of religious districts, which covered about 15.4 percent of the city, was about that of today's suburb of Tama City. And the density of townspeople's districts, which accounted for only 12.5 percent of the total area, was more than three times that of Toshima Ward, which has the highest density in Japan today. The staggering press of humanity was all the greater in that age before high-rise apartments, when many lived in low tenements.

Such tenements filled Nihonbashi, Kanda, Asakusa, Akasaka, and Shiba. Slums began to proliferate at the end of the 18th century, and many from the Kantō and Shinshū (Nagano) regions who came to Edo to find work squatted in these areas. One of these homeless (*yadonashi*) was the great haiku poet Kobayashi Issa (1763–1827). Born on a farm in Kashiwabara in Shinshū, he lost his mother when he was two and left for Edo when he was fifteen, in 1778, spending the next twenty-four years there in poverty:

Even the homeless
observe the Edo
New Year.

A Comparison of the Population Density of Edo and Modern Tokyo   ♠ = 1,000 residents

Edo in 1725
All districts
Density 18,590 residents/km²
(Population 1,300,000; area 69.93 km²)

Warrior districts
Density 13,988 residents/km²
(Population 650,000; area 46.47 km²)

Tokyo in 1980
All Wards
Density 14,109 residents/km²
(Population 8,351,893; area 591.94 km²)

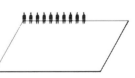

Minato Ward
Density 10,331 residents/km²
(Population 201,257; area 19.48 km²)

178

Niōmon Gate, Sensōji Temple
(see also pp. 86–87)

Townspeople's districts
Density 68,807 residents/km²
(Population 600,000; area 8.72
km²)

Religious districts
Density 4,655 residents/km²
(Population 50,000; area 10.74
km²)

Toshima Ward
Density 22,185 residents/km²
(Population 288,626; area 13.01
km²)

Tama City
Density 4,606 residents/km²
(Population 95,248; area 20.68
km²)

Police chasing a criminal

Evils of City Life

Among Edo's homeless were the inevitable gamblers, thieves, and arsonists. Nezu-mikozō Jirokichi (1797–1832) was one of these so called *narazumono* ("ne'er-do-wells") or *muhōmono* ("outlaws"), famous for his lightning-quick thefts. Though a criminal, he had many admirers, since he stole huge sums from tightly guarded daimyo mansions, then shared it generously with the poor of the slums.

These slums were also ravaged by measles, smallpox, and cholera. One particularly virulent outbreak was the cholera epidemic of 1858, the victims of which often died after only three days, which led to it being called the "three-day death" (*mikka korori*). It was an age when prevention and treatment were almost unknown, and the sick had little to depend on but magic spells or prayers to popular gods. Many entire families were wiped out by the cholera epidemic, and no one dared to go to the baths or barbers. Among the 50,000 to 100,000 victims of the epidemic were the great ukiyoe artist Andō Hiroshige and the popular writer Santō Kyōden (1761–1816).

A smallpox epidemic struck the country in the same year, which prompted Itō Genboku and other students of Western medicine to establish a vaccination clinic in Otamagaike in Kanda. But ingrained prejudices were hard to overcome, and few submitted to inoculation.

Thousands died in the cholera epidemic of 1858

The Arrival of Commodore Perry's Black Ships

In 1853, on the third of the sixth month (July 8 by the Western calendar), four warships led by Commodore Matthew Calbraith Perry anchored off Uraga, southeast of Yokosuka City on the Miura Peninsula. Soon the following verse pillorying fearful shogunal officials was being heard in the streets:

> *Jōkisen*
> wake the nation
> from peaceful sleep—
> only four
> keep everyone up all night!

Here, *jōkisen* (a brand of tea) is played off against its homonym, meaning "steamship," but written with different characters.

The four ships were painted black, and this, plus their great guns, filled those on shore with fear. Messengers immediately left on horseback to report to Edo. An uproar in the streets ensued, with many expecting war with the foreigners to break out any minute. Some loaded their belongings onto carts and sent their children and

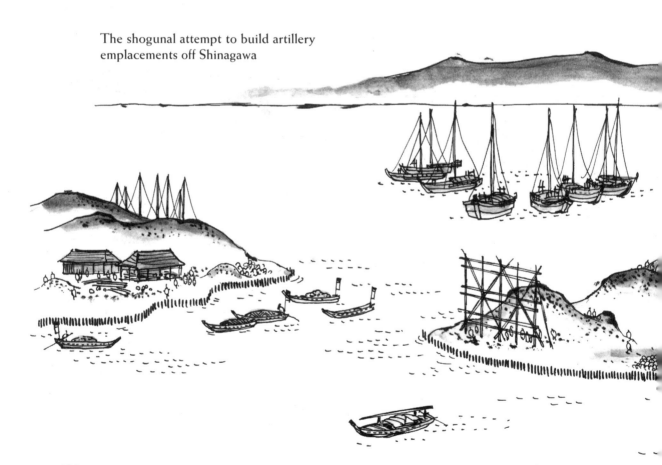

The shogunal attempt to build artillery emplacements off Shinagawa

the aged to safer places outside the city. Panic was heightened by warriors rushing out to buy weapons or answer the call of duty.

Perry had come to demand that the shogunate open the country to foreign trade. On the ninth, carefully watched by warriors from various domains, he disembarked at Kurihama with three hundred marines and personally handed to the magistrate of Uraga a letter to "His Imperial Majesty, the Emperor of Japan" from President Millard Fillmore. He then departed, only to return the next year, on the eleventh of the first month (February 8, 1854), and further panicked the Edoites by sailing this time into the heart of Edo Bay and dropping anchor off Haneda.

Intimidated, the shogunate agreed to negotiations, which were held in the village of Yokohama, outside of Kanagawa on the Tōkaidō Highroad. What resulted, on the third of the third month (March 31), was the Treaty of Kanagawa (*Nichibei washin jōyaku*), which specified that two ports, Shimoda and Hakodate, be opened to American ships. After more than two centuries, Japan's official policy of seclusion had come to an end.

Before the treaty was signed, the shogunate had tried to build artillery emplacements off Shinagawa, using Western engineering designs. The project was overseen by Egawa Hidetatsu, an expert on Western military techniques. Work progressed at a furious pace, but the project was halted before it could be finished due to the signing of the peace treaty.

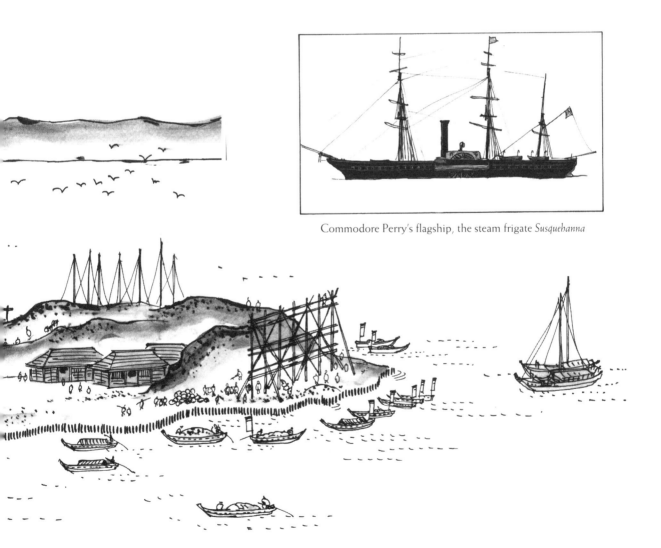

Commodore Perry's flagship, the steam frigate *Susquehanna*

Natural Disasters

The arrival of Commodore Perry was followed by numerous natural disasters, the first of which was an earthquake in 1854, on the fifth of the eleventh month (December 24), that is reckoned to have had a magnitude of 8.4. The size of the quake can be surmised by comparison to the great Kantō earthquake of 1923, of magnitude 7.9, in which more than 100,000 lives were lost. The Japanese coast from the Bōsō Peninsula northeast of Edo all the way down to Kyushu was inundated by tidal waves, and destruction was widespread.

This was followed in the next year, on the first of the tenth month, by bizarre eruptions of ground water throughout Edo, sometimes accompanied by groans from the earth and flashes in the black nighttime sky. The people were aghast and attributed the weird occurrences to evil spirits. Then the next day (November 11, 1855, by the Western calendar) the ground suddenly began to pitch up and down, with a roaring sound like a blast of wind; in a moment even houses built in the sturdy, thick-walled storehouse style collapsed. The epicenter of this great Ansei earthquake, the second massive temblor in two years, was directly below Edo Harbor, and it wreaked havoc in the closely packed Edo neighborhoods. The magnitude is believed to have been 6.9. The devastation was greatest in the downtown areas built on landfill. In the townspeople's districts alone, 14,000 buildings collapsed and 4,000 inhabitants lost their lives. Even in the warrior districts higher up where the ground was firmer, mansions collapsed, killing, among many others, the famous Confucian scholar of the Mito domain Fujita Tōko. Then fire broke out, and even hardened Edoites, inured as they were to conflagrations, feared for their lives.

But this was not the end of natural calamities, for just after the Ansei earthquake, the entire Kantō area was devastated by rains that fell as if the very heavens had opened. Sumidagawa River overflowed and the entire Fukagawa area was flooded. Many felt that it was a demonstration of divine displeasure at a disordered world.

News of the earthquake and flood swept across the nation through hastily printed newspapers (*kawaraban*) and color woodblock prints called "catfish pictures" (*namazue*) from the ancient superstition that earthquakes resulted from the movements of a behemoth catfish that lived underground. Edoites also prayed at Kashima Shrine, famous for its enormous rock formation that went deep into the earth and was thought to have the power to subdue the great fish below.

Before long, the earthquake catfish came to be depicted in human form and to be equated with unscrupulous merchants, who visited their particular calamities on the common population. Such "earthquake men" (*namazuotoko*) were depicted vomiting forth coins to the applause of poor slum dwellers standing by. For many plucky Edoites, the natural disasters portended a millenarian end to evil and the birth of a better world. Such *yonaoshi* ("reform the world") beliefs caught the imagination of more and more Edoites.

Urban Unrest

In 1858 the Great Councilor (Tairō) Ii Nao-suke (1815–60) and the US emissary Townsend Harris (1804–78) signed the first commercial treaty between the United States and Japan, which included the opening of Edo and Osaka for trade. The following year a harbor was built at Yokohama and trade with foreign countries commenced there. Yokohama was conveniently close to Edo, and before long it had surpassed Nagasaki, Japan's only official "window on the west" during the Edo period. Foreign trading houses and banks sprang up, and major firms like Mitsui built outlets there.

Foreign demand for goods, however, inflated prices, as did Japan's revision of its currency, making it harder for townspeople and warriors alike to make ends meet.

Even daimyo suffered, and in 1862 the shogunate relaxed the law of alternate attendance that had so drained daimyo treasuries, and it allowed the lords' women and children to return to their home provinces. As a result of this mass exodus, Edo suddenly lost much of its vitality. Public dissatisfaction with the shogunate increased, and a loyalist movement that was devoted to toppling it and returning actual governing power to the emperor gathered strength. The focus of this movement to "revere the emperor and expel the barbarians" (*sonnō jōi*) was Chōshū (Yamaguchi Prefecture), and the shogunate set out in 1864 to crush the rebels. It initiated a second such campaign the following year, and to provision its army, it bought up huge amounts of rice and other goods. This drove the market price for staples up even further, and public unrest grew greater still. Soon posters started appearing exhorting the people to "smash" (*uchikowashi*) rich establishments.

The first such "smashing" incidents broke out at the Shinagawa waystation. Mobs yelling "Reform! Reform the world!" gathered and broke into rice storehouses, pawn shops, sake stores, and warehouses with foreign goods. The violence then spread across Edo, to Shiba, Ushigome, Yotsuya, Azabu, Akasaka, Kanda, Reiganjima, and Honjo. The latent energy of the masses, so long suppressed, had finally exploded.

The Surrender of Edo Castle

In the tenth month of 1867, the fifteenth Tokugawa shogun, Yoshinobu (also read Keiki, 1837–1913), bowed to the inevitable and officially requested permission to resign, and on the ninth of the twelfth month (January 3, 1868) the emperor declared a return to direct imperial rule. Thus, after two and a half centuries, the Tokugawa regime came to an end.

The spirit of the new age, a mixture of energy, confusion, dedication, and unrest, was symbolized by crowds dancing frenetically and chanting "it's all right" (*ee ja nai ka*). Such dances began in the provinces halfway down the Tōkaidō Highroad then expanded in both directions to Edo and Kyoto. At the same time the second compound of Edo Castle burned. Then early in 1868 troops from the Satsuma, Chōshū, and Tosa (western domains corresponding to today's Kagoshima, Yamaguchi, and Kōchi prefectures) defeated an army of Tokugawa die-hards at the battle of Toba and Fushimi south of Kyoto. At this point the emperor ordered that the campaign against the remnants of the shogunal army be carried to Edo, the heart of the Tokugawa domain. The imperial army thereupon set out east on the Tōkaidō Highroad, flying its brocade imperial banners.

An imperial command to attack Edo Castle itself followed in the third month. Although the abdicated shogun had left the castle and taken refuge in Kan'eiji Temple in Ueno, his troops, the Shōgitai, remained, prepared to do battle. But armed conflict was avoided thanks to a parley between Saigō Takamori (1827–77), representative of the imperial forces, and Katsu Kaishū (1823–99) of the shogunal army, who agreed to hand over Edo Castle to the emperor. The Shōgitai later rose up again, only to be defeated at Ueno that same year.

On the seventeenth of the seventh month (September 3, 1868), Edo was formally renamed the "Eastern Capital," though it is unknown whether the characters for those two words were originally read "Tōkyō" or "Tōkei." Then on the eighth of the ninth month (October 23), the era name was changed to Meiji, with the further stipulation that henceforth there would be only one era name per imperial reign (a system still in effect today). The stage was now set for the monarch known to history as the Meiji Emperor (1852–1912) to set out from Kyoto in the tenth month for the new capital and take up residence in what had been Edo Castle, which was thereupon transformed into the Imperial Palace of today. The old provinces were reorganized into prefectures in 1871, and the next year the Western calendar was adopted. Some decades later the process began to turn the three-hundred-year-old city into the capital of a modern sovereign, and work began on redesigning the city along the lines of Napoleon III's imperial Paris. This marked the start of a new phase in the evolution of old Edo into the Tokyo megalopolis of today.

In the tenth month of 1868, the emperor entered Edo Castle via Gofukubashi Bridge and Wadakuramon Gate.

COMMENTARY

Geography Now and Then

The initial construction of Edo is historically divided into four stages: Stage One, from Tokugawa Ieyasu's entry into Edo in 1590 through 1602, in which the city served as the Tokugawa regional power base in Kantō; Stage Two, from Ieyasu's appointment as shogun in 1603 through the year of his death, 1616, in which the city functioned as the shogunal capital of Ieyasu and his son, Tokugawa Hidetada; Stage Three, from 1617 through the year of Hidetada's death, 1632, in which the city served as the shogunal capital of Hidetada and his son, Tokugawa Iemitsu; Stage Four, from 1633 through the year of Iemitsu's death in 1651, in which the city functioned as Iemitsu's shogunal capital.

Ōta Dōkan

The urban configuration of each of these stages is found in the following maps: Stage One: "Keichō 7 [1602] Map of Edo" (*Keichō shichinen Edo zu, Beppon Keichō Edo zu*); Stage Two: "Keichō 13 [1608] Map of Edo" (*Keichō jūsannen Edo zu, Keichō nenkan Edo zu*); Stage Three: "Map of Edo, Toshimagōri, Musashi Province [Kan'ei 9, 1632]" (*Bushū Toshimagōri Edoshō zu*); Stage Four: "Shōhō Era [1644–48] Pictorial Map of Edo" (*Shōhō nenkan Edo ezu*).

On the endpapers of this book, the Japan Railways (JR) line has been superimposed over these four maps to give a move concrete image of the growth of the city.

The Layout of the Castle and Its Castle Town

In the Edo period, when people referred to a "castle," they generally meant an "inner bastion" (*naikaku*), which consisted of a main compound (*honmaru*), second compound (*ninomaru*), and third compound (*sannomaru*). The surrounding fortified castle town was known by contrast as the "outer bastion" (*gaikaku*). The Japanese name for "compound," *maru*, means "circle," and derives from the practice in the Kamakura period of levelling the top of a hill to serve as a castle foundation. The plan of such castles was necessarily circular in consequence. The main compound was the heart of the castle complex, for it contained the lord's residences and the offices of government. The second compound was for the residences of his children and others closest to him. The third compound was for his most important retainers, and also occasionally for the storage of rice or armaments.

The arrangement of the three compounds was of critical importance. A number of different designs were tried over time, out of which four basic patterns emerged.

Stepped (teikakushiki). In this design, the third compound forms the foundation, atop which the second compound rests, serving in turn as the foundation for the

190

main compound in the highest and most recessed position. This plan is primarily seen in mountain or flatland-hill castles, such as Kumamoto Castle in south Kyushu.

Concentric (kankakushiki). In this design, the main compound is located at the center, forming the apex of a ziggurat with the second and third compounds beneath. This plan is primarily seen in flatland-hill or flatland castles, such as Osaka Castle.

Sequential (renkakushiki). In this design, the main, second, and third compounds are located in a connected line. Though also occasionally seen in flatland-hill castle designs, it is more often seen in flatland castles, such as Takashima Castle in Nagano.

Spiral (kakakushiki). In this design, the second and then the main compound sit above the third compound in spiral fashion. Though also occasionally seen in flatland designs, it is more often seen in flatland-hill castles, such as Edo and Himeji.

Though these four constitute the basic castle plans, two or even three could be combined in a single castle complex. In addition, the largest fortresses might also contain a "countryside compound" (*yamazatomaru*), which included the lord's detached villa, usually located to the north or east for the best view of the moon, and a "west compound" (*nishinomaru*), where the lord would live after he retired from office.

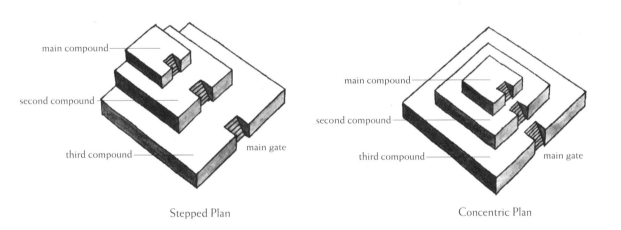

Stepped Plan

Concentric Plan

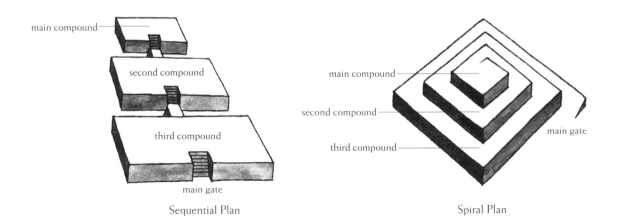

Sequential Plan

Spiral Plan

Wall Construction

It was the stone walls that made the castle what it was, and from the time of Oda Nobunaga's Azuchi Castle, they were the focus of a daimyo's construction efforts. Lords like Katō Kiyomasa employed numerous *anō*, specialists in wall construction.

The stone used was usually igneous rock like andesite or quartz porphyry, plutonic rock like granite, or metamorphic rock like gneiss. In rare cases, marble was used, as at Yatsushiro Castle in Kumamoto Prefecture, or chlorite-schist, as at Wakayama Castle.

There were three basic styles of masonry used once the quarried rock had been delivered to the construction site.

Unfinished (nozurazumi). This style of wall used unfinished stone. It was the oldest method, common in ancient and medieval castle construction. The outer surface of such walls had large gaps between the constituent stones, which made the construction appear weak but actually allowed for efficient rainwater runoff and surprising strength as a result.

Filled (uchikomihagi). This style of wall used unfinished stone faced with finished stone veneer. Smaller stones were used to fill the gaps between the individual blocks. Filled walls became popular after they were used in Oda Nobunaga's Azuchi Castle and were the standard for Momoyama-period walls.

Finished (kirikomihagi). This style of wall used rectangular blocks, cut to a ratio of one by one by two, which produced a surface with almost no gaps. They were set so close that the interstices seemed no more than lines (called *meji*) carved on an otherwise smooth stone surface. The technique for laying the stones in continuous horizontal lines, called *nunozumi* ("cloth coursing"), was perfected in the Edo period. This was the style of finished wall generally used at Edo Castle. Another approach, developed in the mid–Edo period, was to orient the *meji* in a hexagonal or "tortoise shell" (*kikkōzumi*) pattern. Even in the case of unfinished and filled walls, corners were of ashlar blocks cut to a ratio of 1:1:3.

The slope of the walls was normally 67.5 degrees for unfinished walls, 72 degrees for filled walls, and 75 degrees for finished walls (see illustration). But in all three cases, that angle reached the vertical at the top of the wall, the segment called the *tatemizu*. The height of this segment differed according to style. As construction techniques continued to improve, it became possible to build walls so that their upper portions actually bent back outward.

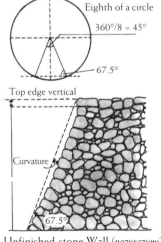

Unfinished-stone Wall (*nozurazumi*)

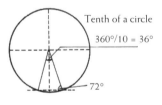

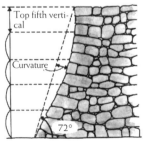

Filled Wall (*uchikomihagi*)

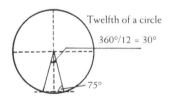

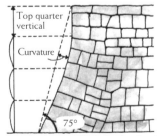

Finished-stone Wall (*kirikomihagi*)

AFTERWORD BY AKIRA NAITŌ

The Tokyo of today gradually evolved out of the Edo of yesterday by applying technological advances as they became available over the years, while at the same time respecting the exigencies of the natural surroundings. At times, too much faith was placed in new architectural advances and urban growth, which was paid for in suffering during earthquakes and fires. But in general the city plan, based on the principle of spiral expansion, was able to successfully respond to changing requirements over time. That plan, alternately followed and amended to allow a degree of free variation, fostered a unique culture, with its kabuki plays and ukiyoe prints, even while living space became extraordinarily dense and confined. Like the times in which it developed, the space combined a feudal control with a degree of spiritual freedom for the least of its residents, and it is this spiritual freedom that must be at the heart of all urban design.

The history of human development, exemplified by the history of Edo, shows that we are not gods, and that we cannot live in or feel joy in a heaven of perfection. Instead, we need urban spaces that also countenance—insofar as they do not cause outright suffering—the dirty, the ugly, and the antiheroic; these too are part of the human make-up. We need cities that reflect the complexity of the human spirit.

The history of the development of Edo, however, is even now not completely understood. I have tried in this book to marshall the most up-to-date scholarship to present that drama in overview. I hope it will stimulate readers to consult the bibliography presented here to pursue the history of Edo in further depth.

I would also like to take this opportunity to acknowledge help received during the writing of this book, particularly from Prof. Kenji Ishii on the history of shipbuilding and from Prof. Yoshio Hattori on the development of kabuki. I am also greatly indebted to my colleague Prof. Kazuo Hozumi for his illustrations and to our editor Reiko Hirayama. I am very grateful to them all.

AFTERWORD BY KAZUO HOZUMI

I must confess that it was with no little trepidation that I first considered illustrating this book, as I doubted it was possible to use pictures to trace the history of not simply a small settlement but of a great metropolis like Tokyo. But as I read through Professor Naitō's manuscript I was increasingly moved by his conceptions and prose style, and so with the encouragement of the editor, Reiko Hirayama, I decided to see what I could do.

I found it both a challenge and an adventure; synthesizing old pictures, screen paintings, and records into a new illustrative form proved very similar to translating ancient texts into the modern vernacular. But despite the difficulties involved, I was excited to be involved in a project of an absolutely new sort, one never attempted by an illustrator before. And yet now, having finished, I find I am more impressed than ever by the skill of the anonymous creators of the screen panoramas of Edo (called *Edo zubyōbu*) of earlier centuries, on whose work I based my own.

Born and raised in downtown Tokyo, I believed I had a special feeling for the old city, but the more I worked on this project, the more I was struck by my ignorance of its history. Climbing Tokyo Tower, strolling through the parks of Ueno or the Imperial Palace, travelling back in time through old maps, and getting to know each small figure in screen paintings, I began to feel that for the first time I was truly coming to grips with the past. That spirit proved to be an enormous motivating force that sustained me through the project, and I am very grateful to have had the experience.

FURTHER READING

In Japanese (compiled by the author)

Unless otherwise indicated, the place of publication is Tokyo.

Akinaga, Yoshirō. *Edo Tōkyō kiba no rekishi* [History of lumber yards in Edo and Tokyo]. Shin Jinbutsu Ōraisha, 1975.

Chiyoda Kuyakusho. *Chiyoda-ku shi* [History of Chiyoda Ward]. Chiyoda-ku, 1960.

Fujiguchi, Tōgo. *Edo hikeshi nendaiki* [Annals of Edo firefighters]. Sōshisha, 1962.

Fujioka, Michio. *Nihon no shiro* [Japanese castles]. Rev. and enl., Shibundō, 1980.

Gotō, Shinpei. *Edo no jichisei* [Edo systems of self-government]. Nishōdō Shoten, 1922.

Haga, Noboru. *Ōedo no seiritsu* [The development of Great Edo]. Yoshikawa Kōbunkan, 1980.

Harada, Tomohiko, Haga Noboru, Moritani Katsuhisa, and Kumakura Isao, ed. *Zuroku toshi seikatsushi jiten* [Illustrated encyclopedia of the history of urban life]. Kashiwa Shobō, 1981.

Hattori, Yukio. *Edo kabuki ron* [On Edo kabuki]. Hōsei Daigaku Shuppankyoku, 1980.

Hayashiya, Tatsusaburō, ed. *Bakumatsu bunka no kenkyū* [Research on Bakumatsu culture]. Iwanami Shoten, 1978.

Hayashiya, Tatsusaburō, ed. *Bunmei kaika no kenkyū* [Research on civilization and enlightenment]. Iwanami Shoten, 1979.

Hayashiya, Tatsusaburō, ed. *Kasei bunka no kenkyū* [Research on Bunka-Bunsei culture]. Iwanami Shoten, 1976.

Hirai, Kiyoshi. *Zusetsu Nihon jūtaku no rekishi* [Illustrated history of Japanese domestic architecture]. Kyoto: Gakugei Shuppansha, 1980.

Hirai, and Kawahigashi Yoshiyuki. *Nihon no shiro* [Japanese castles]. Kin'ensha, 1969.

Horikoshi, Masao. *Nihon no jōsui* [Japanese water systems]. Shinjinbutsu Ōraisha, 1970.

Horikoshi, Masao. *Ido to suidō no hanashi* [Of wells and waterpipes]. Ronsōsha, 1981.

Inagaki, Shisei, ed. *Edo seikatsu jiten* [Dictionary of Edo life]. Seiabō, 1959.

Ishii, Ryōsuke, ed. *Edo machikata no seido* [The layout of Edo]. Jinbutsu Ōraisha, 1968.

Ishii. *Yoshiwara*. Chūō Kōronsha, 1967.

Ishikawa-ken. *Terakoya* [Temple schools]. Shibundō, 1960.

Itō, Teiji. *Minka* [Traditional domestic architecture]. Heibonsha, 1965

Itō. *Shiro—Chikujō no gihō to rekishi* [Castles: The history and technology of castle building]. Yomiuri Shinbunsha, 1973.

Itō, Yoshiichi. *Edo no Yumenoshima* [Edo Yumenoshima]. Yoshikawa Kōbunkan, 1982.

Jinnai, Hidenobu, Itakura Fumio, et al. *Tōkyō no machi o yomu* [Reading the town of Edo]. Sagami Shobō, 1981.

Kaizuka, Sōhei. *Tōkyō no shizenshi* [The history of Tokyo's natural environment]. Kinokuniya Shoten, 1964.

Kawazoe, Noboru. *Tokyo no genfūkei* [The original landscape of Tokyo]. Nihon Hōsō Shuppan Kyōkai, 1979.

Kido, Hisashi. *Senken to itaku* [Sages of the past and their legacy of domestic architecture]. Naka Shoten, 1942.

Kido. *Hangaku kenchiku* [Architecture of fief schools]. Tamba: Yōtokusha, 1945.

Kikuchi, Sansai. *Gohyakunenmae no Tōkyō* [Tokyo five hundred years ago]. Tōkyō Shidankai, 1956.

Kishii, Yoshie, ed. *Edo machizukushi kō* [On the districts of Edo]. Seiabō, 1965.

Kōda, Shigetomo. *Edo to Ōsaka* [Edo and Osaka]. Fuzanbō, 1934.

Konta, Yōzō. *Edo no hon'yasan* [Edo booksellers]. Nihon Hōsō Shuppan Kyōkai, 1977.

Kuki, Shūzō. *Iki no kōzō* [The structure of "iki" (chic)]. Iwanami Shoten, 1930.

Kurata, Nobuo. *Tōkyō no chikasui* [Tokyo's groundwater]. Jitsugyō Kōhōsha, 1962.

Kuroki, Takashi. *Meireki no taika* [The great Meireki fire]. Kōdansha, 1988.

Kusamori, Shin'ichi. *Edo no dezain* [Edo design]. Kyoto: Shinshindō Shuppan, 1972.

Matsuzaki, Toshio. *Edo jidai no sokuryōjutsu* [Measurement in the Edo period]. Sōgō Kagaku Shuppan, 1979.

Minami, Kazuo. *Bakumatsu Edo shakai no kenkyū* [Research on late Edo Society]. Yoshikwa Kōbunkan, 1978.

Minami. *Edo no shakai kōzō* [The social structure of Edo]. Hanawa Shobō, 1969.

Minami. *Ishin zen'ya no Edo shomin* [The Edo townspeople on the eve of the Meiji Restoration]. Higashimurayama: Kyōikusha, 1980.

Mitamura, Engyo. *Edo no fūzoku* [Edo customs]. Daitō Shuppansha, 1941.

Miyao, Shigeo and Kimura Senshū. *Edo shomin machigei fūzokushi* [Popular Edo street entertainment]. Tenbōsha, 1974.

Miyata, Noboru. *Kinsei no hayarigami* [Popular deities in Early Modern Japan]. Hyōronsha, 1972.

Mizue, Renko. *Edo shichū keisei shi no kenkyū* [Research on the history of the urban development of Edo]. Kōbundō, 1977.

Murai, Masuo. *Edōjō* [Edo Castle]. Chūō Kōronsha, 1964.

Naitō, Akira. *Edo to Edojō* [Edo and Edo castle]. Kajima Shuppankai, 1966.

Naitō. *Shiro no Nihonshi* [The history of Japan's castles]. Nihon Hōsō Shuppan Kyōkai, 1979.

Naitō. *Shiro nande mo nyūmon* [Everything about castles]. Shōgakukan, 1980. [For young readers.]

Nakano, Eizō. *Sentō no rekishi* [History of bathhouses]. Yūzankaku Shuppan, 1970.

Nishigaki, Seiji. *Kamigami to minshu undō* [Shinto deities and the democratic movement]. Mainichi Shinbunsha, 1977.

Nishiyama, Matsunosuke. Vol. 1 of *Edo chōnin no kenkyū* [Research on the townspeople of Edo]. Yoshikawa Kōbunkan, 1972.

Nishiyama. *Edokko* [The "child of Edo"]. Yoshikawa Kōbunkan, 1980.

Nishiyama. *Ōedo no bunka* [The culture of Great Edo]. Nihon Hōsō Shuppan Kyōkai, 1981.

Nishiyama, and Haga Noboru, ed. *Edo sanbyakunen—1* [The three hundred years of Edo, part 1]. Kōdansha, 1975.

Nishiyama, and Miyata Noboru, ed. *Edo jidai zushi—Edo 3* [Illustrated Edo: Edo, part 3]. Chikuma Shobō, 1977.

Nishiyama, and Ogi Shinzō, ed. *Edo sanbyakunen—3* [The three hundred years of Edo, part 3]. Kōdansha, 1976.

Nishiyama, and Takeuchi Makoto, ed. *Edo jidai zushi—Edo 2* [Illustrated Edo: Edo, part 2]. Chikuma Shobō, 1976.

Nishiyama, and Takeuchi, ed. *Edo sanbyakunen—2* [The three hundred years of Edo, part 2]. Kōdansha, 1975.

Nishiyama, and Yoshihara Ken'ichirō, ed. *Edo jidai zushi—Edo 1* [Illustrated Edo: Edo, part 1]. Chikuma Shobō, 1975.

Nomura, Kentarō. *Edo*. Shibundō, 1958.

Ogi, Shinzō. *Tōkei jidai: Edo to Tōkyō no aida de* [The "Tōkei" era: The transition from Edo to Tokyo]. Nihon Hōsō Shuppan Kyōkai, 1980.

Ogi. *Tōkyō shomin seikatsu shi kenkyū* [Research in the history of the life of Tokyo townspeople]. Nihon Hōsō Shuppan Kyōkai, 1979.

Ōishi, Shinzaburō. *Edo jidai* [The Edo period]. Chūō Kōronsha, 1977.

Okabe, Seiichi. *Tōkyō tento no shinsō* [The true story of the relocation of the capital to Tokyo]. Jin'yūsha, 1917.

Ōkuma, Yoshikuni. *Edo kenchiku sōwa* [Anecdotes about Edo architecture]. Tōa Shuppansha, 1947.

Ono, Takeo, ed. *Edo no saiji fūzokishi* [Annual events and customs in Edo]. Tenbōsha, 1973.

Ono. *Gōfuku shōnin fūzokushi* [Records of the daily life of wealthy merchants]. Tenbōsha, 1976.

Ōta, Hirotarō. *Jūtaku kindaishi* [History of modern domestic architecture]. Yūzankaku Shuppan, 1969.

Ri'noie, Masafumi. *Kawaya kō* [A study of water closets]. Rokubunkan, 1932.

Sase, Hisashi and Yabe Michinori. *Edo no shoshoku fūzokushi* [Occupations in Edo]. Tenbōsha, 1975.

Suda, Atsuo. *Nihon gekijō shi no kenkyū* [Research on the history of Japan's theaters]. Sagami Shobō, 1957.

Suwa, Haruo. *Edokko no bigaku* [The aesthetics of the "child of Edo"]. Nihon Shoseki, 1980.

Suwa, and Naitō, Akira. *Edozu byōbu* [Edo screen paintings]. Mainichi Shinbunsha, 1972.

Suzuki, Masao. *Edo no kawa, Tōkyō no kawa* [Rivers of Edo, rivers of Tokyo]. Nihon Hōsō Shuppan Kyōkai, 1978.

Suzuki, Toshio. *Edo no hon'ya* [Bookstores of Edo]. Chūō Kōronsha, 1980.

Suzuki, Tōzō and Asakura Haruhiko, ed. *Edo meisho zue* [Famous places in Edo, illustrated]. Kadokawa Shoten, 1966.

Takahashi, Seiichirō. *Edo no ukiyoeshi* [Ukiyoe artists of Edo]. Heibonsha, 1964.

Takahashi, Yōji. "Edo no 'iki'" [Edo chic]. *Bessatsu Taiyō*. Heibonsha, 1981.

Takao, Kazuhiko. *Kinsei no shomin bunka* [Popular culture in early modern Japan]. Iwanami Shoten, 1968.

Takeda, Michiharu. *Sokuryō—Kodai kara gendai made* [Measurement: Its beginnings to the present day]. Kokin Shoin, 1979.

Takeuchi, Yoshitarō. *Nihon gekijō zushi* [Illustrated history of Japanese theaters]. Mibu Shoin, 1935.

Tamai, Tatsurō, ed. *Ukiyoe to chōnin* [Ukiyoe prints and townspeople. Kōdansha, 1982.

Tamamuro, Fumio and Miyata Noboru. *Shomin shinkō no gensō* [Popular beliefs and superstitions]. Mainichi Shinbunsha, 1977.

Teruoka, Yasutaka. *Genroku no enshutsushatachi* [Figures of the Genroku stage]. Asahi Shinbunsha, 1976

Teruoka. *Kōshokumono no sekai, jō, ge* [The world of Saikaku's erotic literature, vols. 1 and 2]. Nihon Hōsō Shuppan Kyōkai, 1979.

Tokyo-to, ed. *Edo no hattatsu* [The development of Edo]. Tokyo-to, 1956.

Tokyo-to, ed. *Toshi kiyō 2: shichū torishimari enkaku, Meiji shonen no keisatsu* [Bulletin of urban history 2: History of law enforcement in the city, the police in the early Meiji period]. Tokyo-to, 1954.

Watanabe, Minoru. *Nihon shokuseikatsushi* [History of dietary habits in Japan]. Yoshikawa Kōbunkan, 1964.

Yoshida, Yoshiaki, ed. *Kiba no rekishi* [History of lumber yards]. Shinrin Shigen Sōgō Taisaku Kyōgikai Gurīn Eiji Henshūshitsu, 1959.

Yoshihara, Ken'ichirō. *Edo no jōhōya* [Edo newsmen]. Nihon Hōsō Shuppan Kyōkai, 1978.

Zenkoku Kōshū Yokujōgyō Kankyō Eisei Dōgyō Kumiai Rengōkai, ed. *Kōshū yokujōshi* [History of public bathhouses]. Zenkoku Kōshū Yokujōgyō Kankyō Eisei Dōgyō Kumiai Rengōkai, 1972.

In English (compiled by the translator)

Ackroyd, Joyce, tr. and commentary. *Lessons from History: The Tokushi Yoron of Arai Hakuseki.* St. Lucia, London, New York: University of Queensland Press, 1982.

Andō, Hiroshige. *One Hundred Famous Views of Edo.* Introductory essays by Henry D. Smith II and Amy G. Poster; commentaries on the plates by Henry D. Smith II. New York: George Braziller, 1986.

Arai, Hakuseki. *Tokushi Yoron.* See Ackroyd.

Arai. *Told Round a Brushwood Fire: The Autobiography of Arai Hakuseki.* Tr., with an introduction and notes, by Joyce Ackroyd. Princeton: Princeton University Press, 1980.

Bashō. See Matsuo Bashō.

Bellah, Robert Neelly. *Tokugawa Religion: The Cultural Roots of Modern Japan.* New York: Free Press, 1985.

Brandon, James R., William P. Malm, and Donald H. Shively. *Studies in Kabuki: Its Acting, Music, and Historical Context*. Honolulu: Institute of Culture and Communication, East-West Center, distributed by University of Hawaii Press, 1978.

Chikamatsu, Monzaemon. *Major Plays of Chikamatsu*. Tr. Donald Keene. New York: Columbia University Press, 1961.

Coaldrake, William H. *Architecture and Authority in Japan*. London and New York: Routledge, 1996.

Coaldrake. "Edo Architecture and Tokugawa Law." *Monumenta Nipponica* 36.3 (Autumn, 1981): 235–84.

Cooper, Michael. *They Came to Japan: An Anthology of European Reports on Japan, 1543–1640*. Berkeley: University of California Press, 1965.

Dalby, Liza Crihfield. *Geisha*. Berkeley: University of California Press, 1983.

Engel, Heino. *The Japanese House: A Tradition for Contemporary Architecture*. Rutland, Vt.: Charles E. Tuttle Co., 1964.

Frost, Peter. *The Bakumatsu Currency Crisis*. Harvard East Asian Monographs 36. Cambridge: Harvard University Press, 1970.

Fujitani, Takashi. *Splendid Monarchy: Power and Pageantry in Modern Japan*. Berkeley: University of California Press, 1996.

Fukuzawa, Yukichi. *The Autobiography of Yukichi Fukuzawa*. Rev. tr. Eiichi Kiyooka. New York: Columbia University Press, 1960.

Gerstle, C. Andrew, ed. *18th Century Japan*. Sydney, Australia: Allen and Unwin, 1989.

Groemer, Gerald. "Dodoitsubō Senka and the *Yose* of Edo." *Monumenta Nipponica* 51.2 (Summer, 1996): 171–87.

Guth, Christine. *Art, Tea, and Industry: Masuda Takashi and the Mitsui Circle*. Princeton: Princeton University Press, 1993.

Guth. *Art of Edo Japan: The Artist and the City, 1615–1868*. New York: H. N. Abrams, 1996.

Guth. *Japanese Art of the Edo Period*. London: Weidenfeld and Nicholson, 1996.

Hall, John Whitney. *Japan: From Prehistory to Modern Times*. Vol. 20 of Delacorte World History. New York: Delacorte Press, 1970.

Hall. *Tanuma Okitsugu, 1719–1788: Forerunner of Modern Japan*. Harvard Yenching Monograph Series 14. Cambridge: Harvard University Press, 1955.

Hall, ed. *The Cambridge History of Japan, Volume 4: Early Modern Japan*. Cambridge: Cambridge University Press, 1991.

Hall and Marius B. Jansen, ed. *Studies in the Institutional History of Early Modern Japan*. Princeton: Princeton University Press, 1968.

Hane, Mikiso. *Peasants, Rebels, and Outcastes: The Underside of Modern Japan*. New York: Pantheon Books, 1982.

Hanley, Susan B. *Everyday Things in Premodern Japan*. Berkeley: University of California Press, 1997.

Hashimoto, Fumio. *Architecture in the Shoin Style: Japanese Feudal Residences*. Tr. and adapted by H. Mack Horton. Vol. 10 of Japanese Arts Library. Tokyo and New York: Kodansha International, 1981.

Havens, Thomas R. H. *Nishi Amane and Modern Japanese Thought*. Princeton: Princeton University Press, 1970.

Hibbett, Howard. *The Floating World in Japanese Fiction*. Rutland, Vt. and Tokyo: Charles E. Tuttle, 1975.

Hinago, Motoo. *Japanese Castles*. Tr. and adapted by William H. Coaldrake. Vol. 14 of Japanese Arts Library. New York and Tokyo: Kodansha International, 1986.

Hirai, Kiyoshi. *Feudal Architecture of Japan*. Tr. Hiroaki Sato and Jeannine Ciliotta. Vol. 13 of The Heibonsha Survey of Japanese Art. Tokyo: Weatherhill / Heibonsha, 1973.

Hirai. *Japanese Domestic Architecture: An Illustrated History*. Tr. Jeffrey Hunter. New York: Weatherhill, 1985.

Hiroshige. See Andō Hiroshige.

Hokusai. See Katsushika Hokusai.

Hur, Nam-lin. *Prayer and Play in Late Tokugawa Japan: Asakusa Sensōji and Edo Society*. Cambridge: Harvard University Asia Center, 2000.

Ihara, Saikaku. *Five Women Who Loved Love*. Tr. William Theodore de Bary. Rutland Vt., and Tokyo: Charles E. Tuttle Co., 1956.

Ihara, Saikaku. *The Life of an Amorous Woman*. Tr. Ivan Morris. New York: New Directions, 1963.

Issa. See Kobayashi Issa.

Itoh, Teiji. *Traditional Domestic Architecture of Japan*. Tr. Richard L. Gage. Vol. 21 of The Heibonsha Survey of Japanese Art. New York: Weatherhill, 1972.

Jansen, Marius B. *Sakamoto Ryōma and the Meiji Restoration*. Stanford: Stanford University Press, 1971.

Jansen, ed. *The Cambridge History of Japan, Volume 5: The Nineteenth Century*. Cambridge: Cambridge University Press, 1989.

Jansen and Gilbert Rozman, ed. *Japan in Transition: From Tokugawa to Meiji*. Princeton: Princeton University Press, 1986.

Jenkins, Donald, ed. *The Floating World Revisited*. Honolulu: University of Hawaii Press, 1994.

Jippensha, Ikku. *Hizakurige or Shank's Mare*. Tr. Thomas Satchell. Rutland, Vt. and Tokyo: Charles E. Tuttle Co., 1960.

Kaempfer, Engelbert. *Kaempfer's Japan: Tokugawa Culture Observed*. Edited, translated, and annotated by Beatrice M. Bodart-Bailey. Honolulu: University of Hawai'i Press, 1999.

Katsushika, Hokusai. *Hokusai: One Hundred Views of Mt. Fuji*. Introduction and commentaries on the plates by Henry D. Smith II. New York: George Braziller, 1988.

Katsushika, Hokusai. *The Hokusai Sketchbooks: Selections from the Manga*. By James A. Michener. Rutland, Vt.: Charles E. Tuttle Co. 1958.

Keene, Donald. *Bunraku: The Art of the Japanese Puppet Theatre*. New York: Kodansha International, 1965.

Keene. *The Japanese Discovery of Europe, 1720–1830*. Palo Alto: Stanford University Press, 1969.

Keene. *World Within Walls: Japanese Literature of the Pre-Modern Era, 1600–1867*. New York: Holt, Rinehart and Winston, 1976.

Kobayashi, Issa. *The Year of My Life: A Translation of Issa's Oraga haru*. Tr. Nobuyuki Yuasa. Berkeley: University of California Press, 1960.

Kracht, Klaus, ed. *Japanese Thought in the Tokugawa Period: A Bibliography of Western-Language Materials*. Wiesbaden: Harrassowitz Verlag, 2000.

Kuki, Shūzō. *Reflections on Japanese Taste: The Structure of Iki.* Tr. John Clark. Ed. Sakuko Matsui and John Clark. Sydney: Power Publications, 1997.

Lane, Richard. *Images from the Floating World: The Japanese Print, Including an Illustrated Dictionary of Ukiyo-e.* New York: Dorset Press, 1978.

Leupp, Gary P. *Servants, Shophands, and Laborers in the Cities of Tokugawa Japan.* Princeton: Princeton University Press, 1992.

Leutner, Robert W. *Shikitei Sanba and the Comic Tradition in Edo Fiction.* Cambridge: Council on East Asian Studies, Harvard University, and the Harvard-Yenching Institute, 1985.

Lidin, Olof G. *The Life of Ogyū Sorai, a Tokugawa Confucian Philosopher.* Scandinavian Institute of Asian Studies Monograph Series 19. Sweden: Studentlitteratur, 1973.

Markus, Andrew L. "The Carnival of Edo: *Misemono* Spectacles from Contemporary Accounts." *Harvard Journal of Asiatic Studies* 45.2 (1985): 499–541.

Maruyama, Masao. *Studies in the Intellectual History of Tokugawa Japan.* Tr. Mikiso Hane. Princeton and Tokyo: Princeton University Press and University of Tokyo Press, 1974.

Matsumoto, Ryōzō, and Eiichi Kiyooka. *Dawn of Western Science in Japan.* Tokyo: Hokuseidō Press, 1969.

Matsuo, Bashō. *The Narrow Road to the Interior.* Tr. Helen Craig McCullough, with Steven D. Carter. In *Classical Japanese Prose: An Anthology*, pp. 522–51. Compiled and edited by Helen Craig McCullough. Stanford: Stanford University Press, 1990.

McClain, James L. *Kanazawa: A Seventeenth Century Japanese Castle Town.* New Haven: Yale University Press, 1982.

McClain, John M. Merriman, and Ugawa Kaoru, ed. *Edo and Paris: Urban Life and the State in the Early Modern Era.* Ithaca: Cornell University Press, 1994.

Michener, James A. *The Floating World.* Honolulu: University of Hawaii Press, 1983.

Miyoshi, Masao. *As We Saw Them: The First Japanese Embassy to the United States (1860).* Berkeley: University of California Press, 1979.

Mizuo, Hiroshi. *Edo Painting: Sotatsu and Korin.* Tr. John M. Shields. Vol. 18 of The Heibonsha Survey of Japanese Art. New York and Tokyo: Weatherhill / Heibonsha, 1972.

Morse, Edward S. *Japanese Homes and Their Surroundings.* Rutland, Vt. and Tokyo: Charles E. Tuttle Co., 1972.

Najita, Tetsuo, and Irwin Scheiner, ed. *Japanese Thought in the Tokugawa Period, 1600–1868: Methods and Metaphors.* Chicago: University of Chicago Press, 1978.

Nakane, Chie, and Ōishi Shinzaburō, ed. *Tokugawa Japan: The Social and Economic Antecedents of Modern Japan.* Tr. edited by Conrad Totman. Tokyo: Tokyo University Press, 1990.

Nishi, Kazuo and Hozumi Kazuo. *What Is Japanese Architecture?* Tr. and adapted, with an introduction, by H. Mack Horton. New York and Tokyo: Kodansha International, 1983.

Nishiyama, Matsunosuke. *Edo Culture: Daily Life and Diversions in Urban Japan, 1600–1868.* Tr. and ed. Gerald Groemer. Honolulu: University of Hawaii Press, 1997.

Nosco, Peter, ed. *Confucianism and Tokugawa Culture.* Princeton: Princeton University Press, 1984.

Okawa, Naomi. *Edo Architecture: Katsura and Nikko.* Photographs by Chuji Hirayama. Tr. Alan Woodhull and Akito Miyamoto. Vol. 20 of The Heibonsha Survey of Japanese Art. New York and Tokyo: Weatherhill / Heibonsha, 1975.

Ooms, Herman. *Charismatic Bureaucrat: A Political Biography of Matsudaira Sadanobu, 1758–1828.* Chicago: University of Chicago Press, 1975.

Ooms. *Tokugawa Ideology: Early Constructs, 1570–1680.* Princeton: Princeton University Press, 1985.

Ōta, Hirotarō, ed. *Japanese Architecture and Gardens.* Tokyo: Kokusai Bunka Shinkokai, 1966.

Paine, Robert Treat, and Alexander Soper. *The Art and Architecture of Japan.* 3rd. ed. Harmondsworth, Middlesex, England: Penguin Books, 1981.

Rozman, Gilbert. "Edo's Importance in the Changing Tokugawa Society." *Journal of Japanese Studies* 1.1 (Spring, 1994): 31–60.

Saikaku. See Ihara Saikaku.

Sakai, Naoki. *Voices of the Past: The Status of Language in Eighteenth-Century Japanese Discourse.* Ithaca: Cornell University Press, 1991.

Sansom, George. *A History of Japan, 1615–1867.* Stanford: Stanford University Press, 1963.

Sansom. *The Western World and Japan: A Study in the Interaction of European and Asiatic Cultures.* New York: Vintage Books, 1949.

Screech, Timon. *The Western Scientific Gaze and Popular Imagery in Later Edo Japan: The Lens Within the Heart.* Cambridge: Cambridge University Press, 1996.

Seidensticker, Edward G. *Low City, High City: Tokyo from Edo to the Earthquake.* New York: Knopf, 1983.

Seidensticker. *Tokyo Rising: The City Since the Great Earthquake.* New York: Knopf, 1990.

Seigel, Cecilia Segawa. *Yoshiwara: The Glittering World of the Japanese Courtesan.* Honolulu: University of Hawaii Press, 1993.

Shikitei, Sanba. See Leutner.

Shively, Donald H. "Sumptuary Regulations and Status in Early Tokugawa Japan." *Harvard Journal of Asiatic Studies* 25 (1964–65): 123–65.

Shogun Age Exhibition Executive Committee, The. *The Shogun Age Exhibition: From the Tokugawa Art Museum.* Tokyo: The Shogun Age Exhibition Executive Committee, 1983.

Smith, Thomas C. *The Agrarian Origins of Modern Japan.* Stanford: Stanford University Press, 1959.

Statler, Oliver. *Japanese Inn.* New York: Pyramid Books, 1962.

Statler. *Shimoda Story.* New York: Random House, 1969.

Statler. *The Black Ship Scroll.* San Francisco and New York: Japan Societies of San Francisco and New York, 1963.

Takahashi, Seiichiro. *Traditional Woodblock Prints of Japan.* Tr. Richard Stanley-Baker. Vol. 22 of The Heibonsha Survey of Japanese Art. New York: Weatherhill: 1972.

Takeda, Izumo, Miyoshi Shōraku, and Namiki Senryū. *Chūshingura: The Treasury of Loyal Retainers.* Tr. Donald Keene. New York: Columbia University Press, 1971.

Totman, Conrad. *Politics in the Tokugawa Bakufu, 1600–1843.* Cambridge: Harvard University Press, 1967.

Totman. *Tokugawa Ieyasu: Shogun.* South San Francisco: Heian International, 1983.

Toyoda, Takeshi. *A History of Pre-Meiji Commerce in Japan.* Tokyo: Kokusai Bunka Shinkokai, 1969.

Tsukahira, Toshio G. *Feudal Control in Tokugawa Japan: The Sankin Kōtai System.* Cambridge: Harvard University Press, 1966.

Vaporis, Constantine Nomikos. *Breaking Barriers: Travel and the State in Early Modern Japan.* Cambridge: Harvard University, Council on East Asian Studies, 1994.

Varley, H. Paul. *Japanese Culture.* 4th ed. Honolulu: University of Hawaii Press, 2000.

Waley, Paul. *Tokyo Now and Then: An Explorer's Guide.* New York: Weatherhill, 1984.

Walthall, Anne. "Peripheries: Rural Culture in Tokugawa Japan." *Monumenta Nipponica* 39.4 (Winter, 1984): 371–92.

Webb, Herschel. *The Japanese Imperial Institution in the Tokugawa Period.* New York: Studies of the East Asian Institute, Columbia University, 1968.

Wigen, Kären. *The Making of a Japanese Periphery, 1750–1920.* Berkeley: University of California Press, 1995.

Yazaki, Takeo. *Social Change and the City in Japan.* Tr. David L. Swain. Tokyo: Japan Publications, 1968.

EDO CHRONOLOGY

Year	Era	Emperor	Shogun	Major Events
1590	Tenshō 18	Goyōzei		Tokugawa Ieyasu takes up residence in Edo Castle after his overlord, Toyotomi Hideyoshi, attains national hegemony by defeating the Hōjō at Odawara
1591	Tenshō 19			Onagigawa River is excavated
1592	Tenshō 20			Edo Castle is repaired; construction begins on the west compound (*nishinomaru*)
1598	Keichō 3			Toyotomi Hideyoshi dies
1600	Keichō 5			Battle of Sekigahara; first Dutch ship arrives in Japan
1601	Keichō 6			Relay system established on the Tōkaidō Highroad
1603	Keichō 8		Ieyasu	Ieyasu appointed shogun; Okuni of Izumo begins performing kabuki in Kyoto; Nihonbashi Bridge built in Edo
1604	Keichō 9			Markers are set at one-league intervals along the five main highroads; major reconstruction plan for Edo castle announced
1605	Keichō 10		Hidetada	Construction begins on Edo Castle and a national corvée is instituted; Ieyasu passes the office of shogun to his son Hidetada
1606	Keichō 11			The shogunal residential palace in the main compound (*honmaru*) of Edo Castle is completed
1607	Keichō 12			The first great keep of Edo Castle is completed
1611	Keichō 16	Gomizunoo		
1612	Keichō 17			The shogunate bans Christianity
1614	Keichō 19			Osaka Winter Campaign
1615	Genna 1			Osaka Summer Campaign; Toyotomi forces defeated; Tokugawa Shogunate enacts its "Regulations for Warrior Households" (*Buke shohatto*)
1616	Genna 2			Ieyasu dies
1617	Genna 3			Yoshiwara made the licensed pleasure quarter
1619	Genna 5			The Higaki guild begins operating the *higaki* cargo ships
1620	Genna 6			Levelling of Kandayama Hill completed; shogunal rice storehouse established in Asakusa
1622	Genna 8			Great keep of Edo Castle rebuilt
1623	Genna 9		Iemitsu	Iemitsu becomes third Tokugawa Shogun
1624	Kan'ei 1			Nakamura Kanzaburō opens a kabuki theater in Nakabashi; Kan'eiji Temple established
1629	Kan'ei 6	Meishō		Ieyasu's great-granddaughter becomes empress.
1634	Kan'ei 11			Families of *fudai* daimyo are moved to Edo; daimyo fire brigades (*daimyōbikeshi*) founded; Iemitsu begins building Nikkō Tōshōgū, the mausoleum of his grandfather Ieyasu
1635	Kan'ei 12			System of alternate attendance (*sankin kōtai*) formulated; Edo Castle outer perimeter constructed
1637	Kan'ei 14			Shimabara Uprising; rebuilding begun on the main compound of Edo Castle; governing system via the "five-family group"

				(*goningumi*) established
1638	Kan'ei 15			Great keep of Edo Castle built a third time
1639	Kan'ei 16			Policy of national seclusion promulgated
1640	Kan'ei 17			Edo Castle completed
1642	Kan'ei 19			Yamamuraza Theater opened in Kobikichō
1643	Kan'ei 20	Gokōmyō		
1650	Keian 3			Major Edo earthquake
1651	Keian 4		Ietsuna	Iemitsu dies; Yui Shōsetsu uprising fails
1654	Jōō 3	Gosai		Tamagawa water system completed
1657	Meireki 3			Meireki fire (Furisode fire); new licensed quarter established near Asakusa
1659	Manji 2			Edo Castle reconstructed; Ryōgoku Bridge built
1663	Kanbun 3	Reigen		
1670	Kanbun 10			Ochikochi Dōin's "Great Map of Edo" published
1673	Enpō 1			Ichikawa Danjūrō I develops the *aragoto* "rough style" of kabuki acting; Mitsui Takatoshi opens the Echigoya store in Edo
1680	Enpō 8		Tsunayoshi	
1683	Tenna 3			Mitsui Takatoshi opens a money exchange in Edo
1684	Jōkyō 1			Shibukawa Shunkai creates the Jōkyō calendar
1686	Jōkyō 3			Saikaku publishes *Five Women Who Loved Love* (*Kōshoku gonin onna*) and *The Life of an Amorous Woman* (*Kōshoku ichidai onna*)
1687	Jōkyō 4	Higashiyama		Tsunayoshi's edicts promulgated on compassion for living things
1689	Genroku 2			Astronomical observatory built at Honjo; Bashō sets out from Edo on the journey eventually published as *The Narrow Road to the Interior* (*Oku no hosomichi*)
1690	Genroku 3			Yushima Seidō Confucian Temple built
1698	Genroku 11			Eitaibashi Bridge built; Naitō Shinjuku waystation established
1702	Genroku 15			Lord Kira's residence attacked by retainers loyal to Lord Asano, a vendetta later staged as *The Treasury of Loyal Retainers* (*Chūshingura*)
1709	Hōei 6	Nakamikado	Ienobu	Tsunayoshi dies; compassion edicts revoked
1712	Shōtoku 2		Ietsugu	
1714	Shōtoku 4			Yamamuraza Theater closed due to the Ejima-Ikushima scandal
1716	Kyōhō 1		Yoshimune	Yoshimune inaugurates the Kyōhō Reforms
1717	Kyōhō 2			Ōoka Tadasuke named south magistrate of Edo
1720	Kyōhō 5			48 town fire brigades established; ban lifted on foreign books entering Japan
1721	Kyōhō 6			Suggestion-box policy inaugurated; Koishikawa Infirmary and Sanatorium built
1726	Kyōhō 11			Daimyo ordered to carry out a domainal census every six years
1732	Kyōhō 17			Great Kyōhō famine
1735	Kyōhō 20	Sakuramachi		
1745	Enkyō 2		Ieshige	
1747	Enkyō 4	Momozono		
1751	Hōreki 1			Yoshimune dies
1760	Hōreki 10		Ieharu	
1762	Hōreki 12	Gosakuramachi		
1764	Meiwa 1			Lending libraries flourish
1765	Meiwa 2			Suzuki Harunobu makes polychrome woodcuts

1770	Meiwa 7	Gomomozono	
1774	An'ei 3		Sugita Genpaku and Maeno Ryōtaku publish *New Book on Anatomy* (*Kaitai shinsho*)
1776	An'ei 5		Hiraga Gennai succeeds in generating electricity
1779	An'ei 8	Kōkaku	
1781	An'ei 10		The woodblock print artist Utamaro begins his career
1783	Tenmei 3		Eruption of Mount Asama; great Tenmei famine
1786	Tenmei 6		Ienari
1787	Tenmei 7		Rice riots in Edo; Matsudaira Sadanobu appointed a Senior Councilor and begins initiating what will become known as the Kansei Reforms
1789	Kansei 1		Tanikaze and Onogawa named sumo grand champions (*yokozuna*)
1790	Kansei 2		Ishikawajima workhouse established; Ansei rustication
1791	Kansei 3		Mixed bathing prohibited
1793	Kansei 5		The Nakamuraza theater installs a revolving stage
1797	Kansei 9		Shōheizaka Academy put under direct shogunal control
1815	Bunka 12		The number of *yose* theaters in Edo reaches 75
1817	Bunka 14	Ninkō	
1821	Bunsei 4		Two camels displayed in Ryōgoku
1832	Tenpō 3		Great Tenpō famine; Nezumikozō Jirokichi captured
1837	Tenpō 8		Ieyoshi
1846	Kōka	Kōmei	
1853	Kaei 6		Iesada	Commodore Perry's Black Ships arrive
1854	Kaei 7		The Treaty of Kanagawa (*Nichibei washin jōyaku*) signed
1855	Ansei 2		Ansei earthquake
1858	Ansei 5		Iemochi	Trade treaty signed; cholera and smallpox rife
1860	Man'en 1		Yokohama port opened to foreign trade
1861	Bunkyū 1		Smallpox vaccinations provided at Otamagaike in Kanda
1862	Bunkyū 2		Requirements relaxed on alternate attendance by daimyo
1863	Bunkyū 3		An elephant displayed in Ryōgoku
1864	Genji 1		First Chōshū campaign
1865	Keiō 1		Second Chōshū campaign
1866	Keiō 2		Yoshinobu	Edo unrest (*uchikowashi*)
1867	Keiō 3	Meiji	Shogun relinquishes ruling power to the emperor
1868	Meiji 1		Edo Castle transferred to the throne; the Shōgitai, the army loyal to the ex-shogun, defeated at Ueno; Edo renamed Tōkyō (perhaps initially read Tōkei)

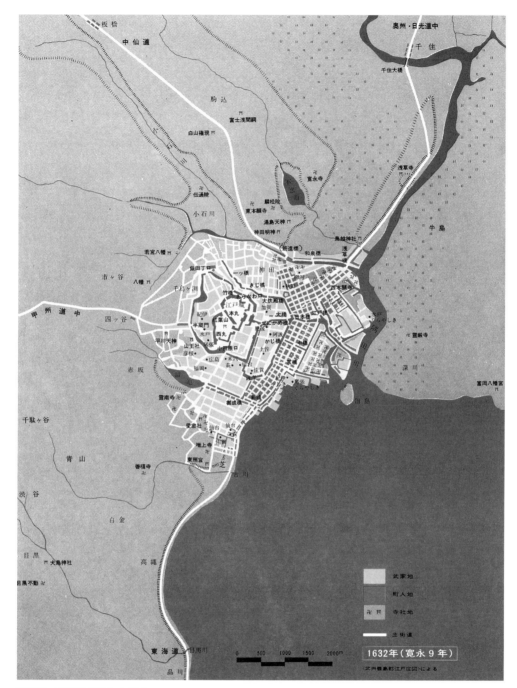

EDO AROUND 1632

From "Map of Edo, Toshimagōri, Musashi Province"
(*Bushū Toshimagōri Edoshō zu*).

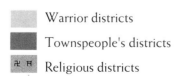 Warrior districts

Townspeople's districts

卍 円 Religious districts

Main Highroads

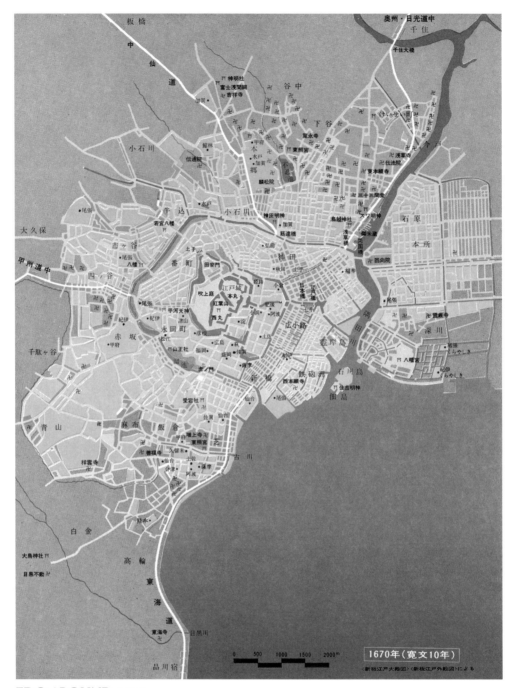

EDO AROUND 1670

From "New Edition of the Great Map of Edo" (*Shinpan Edo Ōezu*) and
"New Edition of the Map of the Environs of Edo" (*Shinpan Edo sotoezu*)

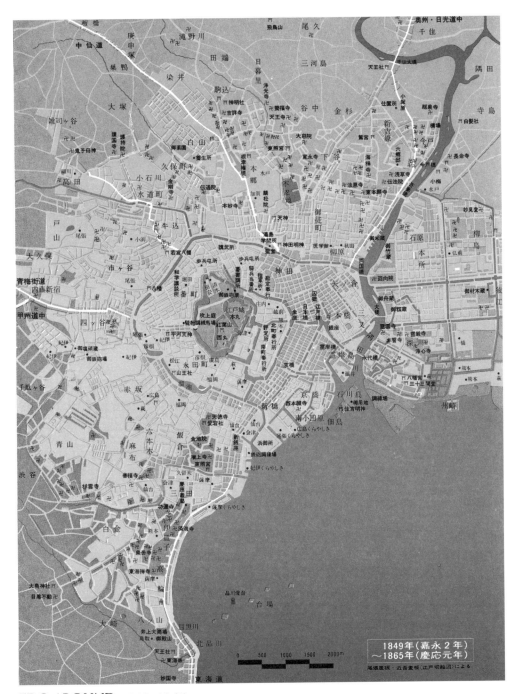

EDO AROUND 1849-1865

From the Owariya and Kongōdō editions of "The Kirie Map of Edo"
(*Owariya-ban, Kongōdō-ban "Edo kiriezu"*)

INDEX

江戸の町
EDO, THE CITY THAT BECAME TOKYO

2003 年 4 月11日　第 1 刷発行

著　者　　内藤　昌／穂積和夫
訳　者　　マック・ホートン
発行者　　畑野文夫
発行所　　講談社インターナショナル株式会社
　　　　　〒112-8652 東京都文京区音羽 1-17-14
　　　　　電話　03-3944-6493（編集部）
　　　　　　　　03-3944-6492（営業部・業務部）
　　　　　ホームページ　http://www.kodansha-intl.co.jp
印刷所　　大日本印刷株式会社
製本所　　黒柳製本株式会社

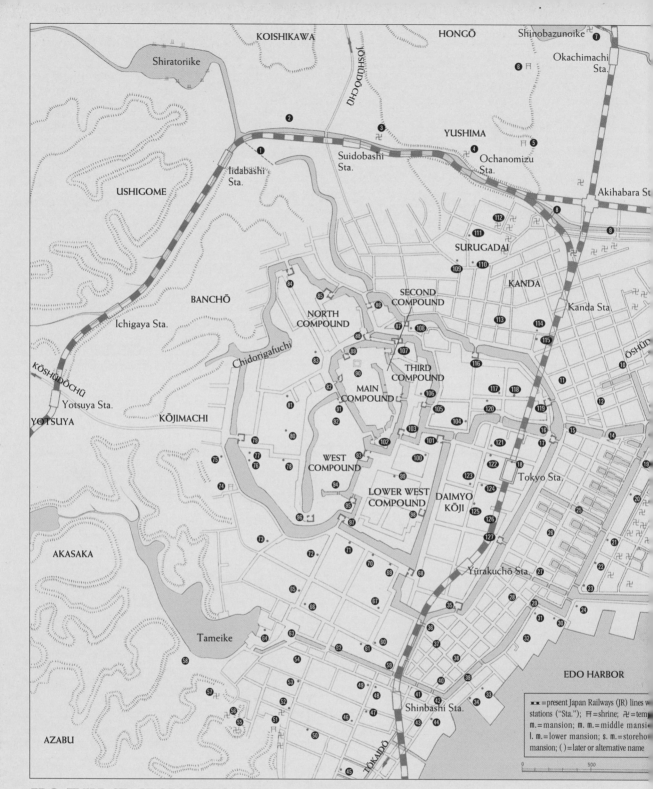

EDO: THIRD STAGE OF DEVELOPMENT (CA. 1632). From "Map of Edo, Toshimagōri, Musashi Province [Kan'ei 9, 1632]" (*Bushū Toshimagōri Edoshō*

1. Rerouting Hirakawa; 2. Mito l. m.; 3. Kichijōji; 4. Kōrinji; 5. Kanda Myōjin; 6. Yushima Tenjin; 7. Kan'eiji; 8. Sujikaibashi; 9. Kandagawa; 10. Ōdenmachō; 11. Honchō; 12. Muromachi; 13. Edobashi; 14. Nihonbashi; 15. Ikkokubashi; 16. Zenigamebashi; 17. Gotōbashi (Gofukubashimon); 18. Mori Mimasaka; 19. Takahashi (Kaizokubashi); 20. Kuki l. m.; 21. Matsudaira Nakatsukasa m. m.; 22. Torii m. m.; 23. Shimada l. m.; 24. Honda Shimousa l. m.; 25. Nakabashi; 26. Minamidenmachō; 27. Kyōbashi; 28. Shinryōgaechō (Ginza); 29. Kinokunibashi; 30. Owari s. m.; 31. Kii s. m.; 32. Kobikichō; 33. Matsudaira Suō l. m.; 34. Matsudaira Echigo s. m.; 35. Sukiyabashimon; 36. Yamashitabashi; 37. Kagachō; 38. Owarichō; 39. Sanjukkenbori; 40. Izumochō; 41. Namidabashi; 42. Shinbashi; 43. Hibiyachō; 44. Wakisaka l. m.; 45. Date m. m.; 46. Mori Nagato l. m.; 47. Mōri l. m.; 48. Wakisaka m.; 49. Akizuki m.; 50. Kyōgoku Wakasa m.; 51. Atago; 52. Sakuma l. m.; 53. Hosokawa Sansai m.; 54. Kubochō; 55. Kōgakuin; 56. Sengakuji; 57. Reinanji; 58. Yakatachō; 59. Onaribashi; 60. Shimazu m.; 61. Sagara m.; 62. Dobashi (Atarashibashi); 63. Toranomon; 64. Naitō m.; 65. Kuroda m.; 66. Kanamori m.; 67. Nabeshima m.; 68. Hibiyamon; 69. Date m.; 70. Mōri m.; 71. Uesugi m.;

72. Asano m.; 73. Ii m.; 74. Hiyoshi Sannō; 75. Matsudaira Echigo m.; 76. Takekoshi m.; 77. Naruse Owari m.; 79. Kōjimachiguchi (Hanzōmon); 80. Mito m.; 81. Kii m.; 82. Nishihanebashimon; 83. Suru 84. Iidamachiguchi (Tayasumon); 85. Shimizumon; 86. Kijibashimon; 87. Hitotsubashimo Takebashimon; 89. Kitahanebashimon; 90. keep; 91. Yamashitamon; 92. Momijiyama; 93. Sakashita 94. Nijūbashi; 95. Nishinomaruōtemon; 96. Fukiagemon; 97. Odawaraguchi (Sotosakuradamor Babasakimon; 99. Honda Kai m.; 100. Matsudaira Shikibu m.; 101. Wadakuramon; 102. Hasuikemo Uchisakuradamon; 104. Matsudaira Iyo m.; 105. Ōhashiguchi (Ōtemon); 106. Sakai Gagaku m Hirakawamon; 108. Matsudaira Izu m.; 109. Matsudaira Shimousa m.; 110. Tsugaru m.; 111. Kobori T m.; 112. Kannon'in; 113. Mikawachō; 114. Satake m.; 115. Inoue Shin'emon l. m.; 116. Ōidonc (Kandabashimon); 117. Tōdō m.; 118. Ikoma m.; 119. Ōhashi (Tokiwabashimon); 120. Maeda m Hosokawa Etchū m.; 122. Hachisuka m.; 123. Ikeda m.; 124. Arima m.; 125. Kyōgoku Tango m.; 126. Koi 127. Kajibashimon